THE REMOTE WORKER'S GUIDE TO TIME MANAGEMENT

SAM BYTE

PILAR ORTI

COLLECTIVE WISDOM

Copyright © 2024 by Pilar Orti

Print ISBN: 978-0-9572802-7-4

All rights reserved.

No part of this book may be reproduced in any form or by any electronic or mechanical means, including information storage and retrieval systems, without written permission from the author, except for the use of brief quotations in a book review.

Images: Pilar Orti

Cover image: DALL-E

Cover design: Pilar Orti, created in Canva

Disclaimer

This book is intended for informational purposes only. The author and publisher are not responsible for any actions taken by the reader based on the material in this book. While efforts have been made to ensure accuracy, the author and publisher make no warranties about the book's content and disclaim liability for any direct or indirect consequences of its use.

Please use your common sense.

❀ Created with Vellum

CONTENTS

Foreword	vii
Introduction	ix

PART 1: FOUNDATIONS — 1

1. FOUNDATIONS AND MYTHS OF TIME MANAGEMENT — 3
- Embracing Flexibility and Adaptability — 4
- No Size Fits All — 7
- Quick Content Summary — 7
- Productivity Pathfinders — 8

2. PROCRASTINATION — 9
- Understanding Procrastination: Defining the Challenge — 10
- Mindset Traps Leading to Procrastination — 11
- Distractions: The Gateway to Procrastination — 15
- Multitasking as a Procrastination Tactic — 17
- Remote Work is Not Just "Working from Home" — 19
- Short-Term Tactics to Combat Procrastination — 20
- Quick Content Summary — 21
- Productivity Pathfinders — 22

3. SEPARATING WORK FROM "LIFE" - OR NOT — 23
- Separators and Integrators — 24
- Work-Life Dynamics — 29
- Your "Work-Life" Relationship — 31
- Quick Content Summary — 33
- Productivity Pathfinders — 33

4. YOUR PHYSICAL ENVIRONMENT AND RESOURCES — 35
- Crafting Your Ideal Workspace — 35
- Personalising Your Space — 37
- A Spot Fit for Meetings — 39
- Essential Tools and Technology for Remote Work — 41
- Quick Content Summary — 43
- Productivity Pathfinders — 43

PART 2: TACTICS AND STRATEGIES — 45

5. PLANNING AND REVIEWING ROUTINES — 47
- Crafting the First Hours of Your Day — 47
- Finding Clarity and Creativity through Free Writing — 49
- The Unsung Hero of Productivity: the 'Not To-Do List' — 50
- Ending your Day — 51
- A Structured End of Day Routine — 52
- Quick Content Summary — 54
- Productivity Pathfinders — 54

6. POPULAR TIME MANAGEMENT AND PLANNING TECHNIQUES — 55
- The Eisenhower Matrix — 55
- The Pomodoro Technique — 57
- The 90-Minute Work Cycle for Deep Focus — 58
- Time Blocking and Task Batching — 59
- Manager vs Maker — 60
- The Remote Work Add-on: Synchronous vs Asynchronous Tasks — 62
- Quick Content Summary and Productivity Pathfinders — 64

7. LESS POPULAR TIME MANAGEMENT STRATEGIES — 65
- Defining Your Boundaries — 65
- When to Say "No" and How — 68
- Templates for Saying "No" to Others — 68
- Saying "No" to Yourself — 70
- Nurturing Your Professional Relationships — 71
- Quick Content Summary — 73
- Productivity Pathfinders — 73

PART 3: TECHNOLOGY — 75

8. NAVIGATING DIGITAL TOOLS FOR INDIVIDUAL PRODUCTIVITY — 77
- The Quest for the Perfect Productivity Tool — 77
- Essential Types of Digital Tools — 81
- Project Management Tools — 82
- Time Tracking: Beyond the Clock — 84
- Quick Content Summary — 86
- Productivity Pathfinders — 86

9. CONTROL THE TECH BEFORE IT CONTROLS YOU — 89
- A Quartet of Communication Essentials — 89
- Avoiding External Interruptions — 91
- The Dangers of Digital Presenteeism — 94
- Identifying the Symptoms of Burnout — 95

Quick Content Summary	97
Productivity Pathfinders	97
PART 4: TRANSFORMATION	99
10. PROGRESS AND TRANSFORMATION	101
The Essence of Ongoing Development	102
Journaling for Growth	105
Conducting a Weekly Review	107
Future-Proofing Your Remote Work Experience	108
Final Words	109
Quick Content Summary	110
A Final Call to Action	110
References	111
Acknowledgments	113
About Pilar Orti and Sam Byte	117

FOREWORD

A WORD FROM THE HUMAN CO-AUTHOR

Hi, I'm Pilar Orti, the human author. Sam Byte is the pen name I've created for my AI co-author.

I've been in the field of remote work for almost a decade now, helping managers of remote teams change their leadership styles to better suit this relatively new way of working. Along the way, I've paid attention to the struggles faced by managers and their teams, as well as to the spectrum of advice offered by experts on evergreen topics like time management, motivation, loneliness and emotional intelligence.

What I love most about working in the 'world of work' field is that the answer to most "How do I…?" questions is "It depends".

And as a writer, trainer, consultant, and presenter I also find that my own response to most "How do I" questions is also, "It depends". Which makes me a poor writer of How-To books.

That's why I've turned to Generative AI, particularly ChatGPT, to help me write this book. ChatGPT can synthesise a large amount of data and summarise it concisely. It does this by predicting the most likely word sequences, drawn from data mainly obtained from the internet. Considering the vast amount of material available online on topics like 'time management for remote workers', you can see how, with the right prompts, ChatGPT can present a broad and comprehensive vision of the topic.

My own knowledge of time management is also broad, but it's not my main area of expertise. I've read a lot on the topic (who hasn't!) but, more importantly, I've always read it with a critical eye. I scrutinise 'best practices' and carefully examine the origins and research behind one-dimensional advice. It's through this lens that I have guided and edited the material generated by ChatGPT.

This book is a co-creation between human and machine. Sam Byte is the name I've given to the collection of AI tools I use, including those which generate words. My own input has been key in presenting a piece of work that I hope will be useful to many fellow remote workers.

I've done my best to challenge the narratives of 'remote work is working from home' and one-size-fits-all advice. I've aimed to polish the style to give you a mixture of down-to-earth advice and aspirational insights that I know is key for inspiring change.

This is a book I couldn't have written on my own - and it's a book I hope will help us continue to show that remote work does indeed work.

Pilar Orti

London, January 2024

INTRODUCTION

The concept of time management at work transcends the confines of office walls and traditional work hours. "The Remote Worker's Guide to Time Management" is an exploration of principles, strategies, and practices tailored for those who seek to convert the comfort of their chosen workspaces into sanctuaries of efficiency and creativity.

You, the reader, are the modern-day knowledge-worker, principally but not exclusively working from home, navigating the waters of remote work with the determination to succeed. You might be at the outset of this journey, seeking guidance, or perhaps you're further along, looking to refine your methods. This book is for the self-starters, those who are willing to take charge of their time and craft a work-life rhythm that resonates with their personal and professional aspirations.

Divided into four parts, this guide unfolds progressively, starting with **foundational concepts of time management** in Part 1. Part 2 is full of practical advice for **day-to-day task prioritisation and boundary setting**, while Part 3 tackles the digital realm, equipping you to **harness technology without becoming its servant**.

The final section, Part 4, is an invitation to turn what you have learned into a **commitment of ongoing self-development** - a celebration of progress and a call to action for continuous improvement. Throughout the book, you'll find the clarity of actionable advice, and the encouragement to excel in your work.

HOW TO USE THIS BOOK

Take a look at the Table of Contents. It's designed to help you identify the areas where you feel you need the most guidance or insight. I also encourage you to read the book in its entirety. Sometimes the knowledge or tips that can have the greatest impact on your work life are found in the chapters you might not initially consider relevant. Remember, you don't know what you don't know until you discover it.

Make notes as you read along. Highlight those sections that offer valuable reminders and insights for the future. Jot down ideas and strategies you'd like to experiment with or implement in your own routine.

If you prefer a more structured approach to applying the insights gained from this book, read carefully through the Productivity Pathfinders at the end of each chapter. These calls to action are designed to help you to turn the concepts and strategies discussed into tangible improvements in your daily work life. While you may find value in all of these suggestions, consider implementing one or two that specifically address your immediate needs or challenges. Over time, you can gradually incorporate additional Pathfinders to further refine and improve your productivity.

Along the way, I've also included well-known (and lesser known) quotes that neatly summarise the concepts and calls to action of the book. Here's the first of such quotes to move us into the first part of the book:

 "The secret of getting ahead is getting started." - attributed to Mark Twain

So let's begin.

Sam Byte, January 2024

PART 1: FOUNDATIONS

CHAPTER 1
FOUNDATIONS AND MYTHS OF TIME MANAGEMENT

"In the office, my day revolved around meetings, coffee breaks with colleagues, and an unspoken rule: pack up when everyone else does. Working from home, suddenly I had all this flexibility, but no framework to structure it. It was freeing yet disorienting."

These words echo the experiences of many remote workers, particularly those who began their careers in traditional office environments and later transitioned to remote work, often from home. Remote work can easily blur the lines between professional and personal life, bringing both opportunities for freedom and challenges in managing your time.

The initial shift to remote work can feel euphoric: no commutes, flexible schedules, and the ability to choose where you work. Yet, it soon becomes clear that this freedom requires greater self-discipline and regulation. The absence of external cues – like the bustling energy of an office or the physical presence of colleagues – means that remote workers must internalise time management in a way they never had to before.

A new form of discipline

Transitioning to remote work introduces a range of challenges and adjustments, particularly in how we discipline ourselves in an environment without the physical and social structures of an office.

One of these challenges, also shared by other knowledge workers, is the overlap of devices for professional and personal use, like social media, streaming, and other online distractions. Without a physical shift from office to home, the end of the workday can blur, potentially leading to extended work hours and the risk of burnout.

Remote work also shifts the focus from visible activity, as seen in office environments, to actual output and results. This emphasises the importance of genuine productivity over mere presence, challenging traditional notions of what it means to be productive.

In addition to this, for those who regularly collaborate with others, there is a need to be more intentional about communication. While a quick chat in the office corridor can easily resolve issues or spark ideas, remote interactions demand more planning and a delicate balance between real-time discussions and asynchronous communication. This shift can be challenging for some, requiring an adjustment in how they approach and manage their interactions.

Bearing in mind the above challenges, let's turn to the set of principles that underpin every strategy, technique, and tool presented in this book. Think of them as the mental groundwork necessary for building a more productive, balanced, and fulfilling work life. As you turn these pages, keep an open mind to these core principles — they are the first step in transforming the way you work.

EMBRACING FLEXIBILITY AND ADAPTABILITY

Unlike traditional office environments with set routines, remote work can involve varying schedules, fluctuating workloads, and unexpected demands. Adopting a flexible mindset means being prepared to adjust your methods and routines in response to these changes. It's about finding the balance between having a structured plan and being open to modifying it as situations evolve. This flexibility can be a significant asset in managing your time effectively, ensuring that you remain productive and efficient, even when the unexpected happens.

Quality over quantity

There's a common misconception that being busy equates to being productive. However, effective time management isn't about filling every minute of your day with tasks; it's about prioritising and focusing on tasks that offer the most significant value. This is especially relevant in remote work, where self-imposed pressure to constantly perform can lead to burnout. By concentrating on quality, you can ensure that your time is spent on activities that truly matter and contribute to your overall objectives.

 "The key is in not spending time, but in investing it." – Stephen R. Covey

Self-awareness and personalisation

There is no universal solution for managing time effectively. Each individual has their unique rhythms, work styles, and productivity peaks. The key is to recognise your own patterns and tailor your time management strategies to fit your personal style. This might involve scheduling demanding tasks during your peak productivity periods and saving less intensive tasks for times when your energy is lower. Personalising your approach helps you to work in harmony with your natural tendencies, not against them.

Balancing professional tasks and personal wellbeing

The inherent flexibility of remote work, while advantageous, can sometimes lead to blurred boundaries, making it difficult to disengage and relax. Effective time management goes beyond just organising work tasks; it equally involves consciously carving out time for rest and activities that rejuvenate your mind and body. This holistic approach ensures that your pursuit of professional productivity is balanced with nurturing your overall well-being, creating a sustainable work-life rhythm that supports both career success and personal fulfilment.

Protecting your time

One of the dangers of working remotely is that others might perceive that, as you can work from multiple devices, and your work is done online, you are available at all times. We know that extended working hours often lead to decreased productivity, not to mention the potential for burnout. Just as athletes need downtime for muscle recovery, knowledge workers need breaks for mental recovery. Extended working hours can lead to mental fatigue, reducing cognitive function and creativity. It's like trying to squeeze more juice out of an already squeezed lemon – at some point, there's just no juice left.

Defining and defending your time boundaries becomes even more important when your communication with others is done online - we'll look at this in Chapter 7.

 "The trouble is, you think you have time." – Buddha

Adopting a learning mindset

Improving your time management involves being open to trying new strategies, tools, and methods, and assessing their effectiveness in your work life. This continuous learning process also involves being reflective, regularly assessing your productivity, and being honest about what is and isn't working.

As a remote worker, this journey is deeply linked with self-discipline. Without the conventional frameworks and direct supervision typical of office environments, the onus falls on you to proactively manage your self-assessment and learning journey.

NO SIZE FITS ALL

You might have read about the importance of sticking to a rigid schedule, like traditional office hours, as the key to success when working from home. But for some people, forcing yourself to follow a 9-to-5 routine while working remotely can be as out of place as wearing a suit to a beach party. You might thrive on a strict schedule, or you might find that a more fluid approach suits your lifestyle and work rhythm better. Remote work gives you the freedom to adjust your schedule, whether you're an early bird or a night owl. It acknowledges that your peak productivity hours can differ significantly. The goal is to find a rhythm that matches your internal clock, your tasks and your collaborations, not to stick to a one-size-fits-all routine.

The same goes for the belief that dressing up boosts productivity in a home environment. Sure, wearing business attire can help some transition into 'work mode' and maintain a professional mindset. But it's not a universal solution. Comfort might be more important for you, and you might find you work best in your pyjamas. Thinking you need to dress up to be productive at home is like saying you must wear gym attire to feel fit. It's the quality of your work, not your outfit, that really matters. The freedom to choose what you wear is one of the perks of working remotely, whether you're working from home or a coworking space of your choice.

But remember that when you have video meetings, either with colleagues or external clients, what you wear still matters. In these situations, you'll need to choose an outfit that's appropriate, at least from the waist up.

∼

QUICK CONTENT SUMMARY

- Transitioning from office to remote work and its impact on time management.

- Quality over quantity, self-awareness and personalisation as key principles.
- Balancing professional tasks with personal well-being and adopting a learning mindset.

PRODUCTIVITY PATHFINDERS

Here is your first set of 'Productivity Pathfinders'.

Start by selecting one or two that directly address your current challenges.

1. Reflect on Your Work Patterns: How does the absence of external time cues, like the end of the office day, affect your productivity and work-life dynamic? Reflect on your daily routine and identify times when you are most and least productive.
2. Experiment with Flexibility: This week, adjust your schedule in small ways to better accommodate unexpected tasks or changes in workload.
3. Focus on Quality: For the next few days, consciously prioritise tasks that add significant value to your work, rather than trying to fill every minute.

CHAPTER 2
PROCRASTINATION

In Chapter 2, we confront the challenge of procrastination, particularly as it manifests in the remote work environment. We dissect the psychological underpinnings of procrastination, illustrating how our own cognitive biases can hinder our progress.

Understanding procrastination is more than recognising a bad habit; it's about acknowledging the complex interplay of emotions and thoughts that lead us to avoid tasks. By recognising these internal obstacles, we can develop strategies to counteract them, adopt a more realistic approach to our work, and ultimately break the cycle of procrastination.

We'll also consider the role of our environment and the potential of 'third spaces' such as coworking spaces and cafés in mitigating procrastination.

In addressing procrastination, this chapter goes beyond simple time management tips. It aims to equip you with the understanding and tools needed to manage not only your schedule but also your mindset, paving the way for more disciplined and efficient work habits.

 "The most difficult thing is the decision to act, the rest is merely tenacity." – Amelia Earhart

UNDERSTANDING PROCRASTINATION: DEFINING THE CHALLENGE

Everyone was surprised by the high levels of productivity reported during the mandatory work-from-home periods during the coronavirus pandemic. For decades, it was widely believed that the home environment, filled with its own distractions, would encourage procrastination. However, this period demonstrated that with the right approach and mindset, remote work could be just as, if not more, productive than traditional office settings.

Procrastination is the act of delaying or postponing tasks and it has been proved to be more common among those who work from home. A study by Tice and Baumeister (1997) suggests that procrastination is often a way of coping with challenging emotions and stressful tasks. Without the structured environment of an office, home workers might find it easier to give in to distractions as a means of avoiding these uncomfortable feelings. The absence of direct oversight and immediate accountability, as well as the absence of interpersonal distractions, can further exacerbate this. It's like avoiding a doctor's visit for fear of bad news; the delay is a temporary escape from facing potential challenges or stressors.

For those with perfectionist tendencies, unstructured environments present even more of a challenge. Gordon L. Flett and colleagues in their 2012 study, suggest that individuals with perfectionist tendencies might procrastinate more in settings where they feel less structured, as they fear not meeting their high standards. In the comfort of one's home, where perfectionist pressures might feel more pronounced due to the lack of immediate feedback, remote workers may fall into the trap of postponing work, ironically, in an effort to do it 'perfectly' later.

While these studies offer valuable insights, you need to remember that the dynamics of procrastination can be complex and varied. The reasons behind procrastination can differ greatly from one individual to another, influenced by personal habits, work environment, psychological factors, and even aspects of one's personal life.

The important thing is to see that the first step towards combating procrastination is to recognise it - understanding the psychological underpinnings can be a helpful tool in developing strategies to overcome it.

MINDSET TRAPS LEADING TO PROCRASTINATION

Meet Alex, a graphic designer who has recently started a new project, redesigning a website for a major client. The client expects a complete overhaul of their existing site, incorporating modern design elements, responsive layouts, and interactive features. Every time Alex thinks about the project, they imagine failing to meet the client's expectations, leading to negative feedback and damage to their professional reputation. This fear makes Alex anxious and hesitant to begin work, despite a track record of successful web design. We call this cognitive bias '**catastrophising**'.

As a result, Alex's project sits like a mountain on his to-do list, getting continually pushed back as our graphic designer tells himself, "I'll be more prepared to tackle it tomorrow." This is the '**optimism bias**' at play, where Alex overestimates his future productivity, not accounting for the likelihood that his emotional response to the task will remain the same.

Alex will be ok in the future, don't worry, so let's turn our attention to Emily, a content writer. She often finds herself saying, "Oh, writing this article will only take a couple of hours," but in reality, it takes much longer. This misjudgment leads to a domino effect of procrastination, as tasks pile up, making her feel overwhelmed. The overwhelm then triggers an emotional response of avoidance, and she finds herself cleaning her already spotless apartment or baking third batches of cookies – anything but writing. All because of the '**planning fallacy**', a cognitive bias where she underestimates the time required to complete a task

Cognitive biases, which are the subconscious influences on our thinking and decision-making, and emotional responses intertwine to fuel procrastination. In Alex's case, the interplay of catastrophising and optimism bias creates a cycle of anxiety and postponement. For Emily, the planning fallacy leads to an unrealistic schedule, resulting in stress and avoidance behaviours. Time management is not just about managing time; it's also about managing one's mindset and emotional reactions to tasks. By acknowledging and addressing these internal hurdles, you can take a more realistic and effective approach to your work, breaking the cycle of procrastination.

Do you ever experience what Alex or Sarah go through?

Catastrophising: Imagining and believing the worst possible outcome of a situation.

Optimism bias: The tendency to overestimate the likelihood of positive outcomes.

Planning fallacy: Underestimating the time required to complete tasks, often leading to overly optimistic time frames.

There are other biases that affect our productivity and how we approach our work. Being aware of them can help us redirect our efforts. Do you ever fall into any of these?

The present bias

The tendency to prioritise immediate rewards over future benefits. Imagine that you choose to watch a new episode of your favourite series instead of progressing on a lengthy report due next week. In your mind, the immediate gratification from relaxing and watching TV outweighs the future benefit of completing the report. The present bias often leads to last-minute rushes and heightened stress, as long-term projects are consistently nudged aside for short-term pleasures.

The perfectionism trap

While not a cognitive bias in the traditional sense, perfectionism can lead to procrastination, especially in remote settings where self-imposed standards are unchecked. For example, a freelance writer might spend an excessive amount of time perfecting an article, leading to a delayed submission and hindering their ability to take on additional work. This pursuit of perfection can lead to a cycle of constant revisions and delays, as the work never seems 'good enough'.

The Dunning-Kruger effect

Named after psychologists David Dunning and Justin Kruger, this bias refers to the overestimation of one's abilities, leading to underestimating the time and effort a task requires. You might assume a project is straightforward and so delay starting it, only to find later that it's more complex than you initially thought. This can lead to rushing through the work at the last minute, and decreasing the quality of the work.

The sunk-cost fallacy

This occurs when individuals continue a behaviour or endeavour as a result of previously invested resources (time, money, or effort), even if the current costs outweigh the benefits. For example, a marketing consultant might spend hours on a promotional strategy that isn't yielding results. Instead of pivoting or abandoning the ineffective strategy, he keeps at it, thinking about the time already invested. This fallacy can lead to procrastination on making necessary changes or starting new, more effective tasks because of the fixation on recouping lost investments.

Finding and facing your biases

To effectively use the knowledge of these biases in your work day and planning, consider implementing the following call-to-action steps:

1. **Reflect and acknowledge**: Start by acknowledging the presence of these biases in your daily work. Regular self-reflection can help you identify patterns of behaviour that align with these biases. Awareness is the first step towards change.

2. **Set realistic goals and deadlines**: Counteract the planning fallacy and present bias by setting realistic and achievable goals (yes, this is easier said than done!). Break down large tasks into smaller, manageable steps with clear, attainable deadlines. This can help maintain focus and reduce the allure of immediate, less productive activities.

3. **Develop a balanced perspective**: To address catastrophising, practice balancing negative thoughts with realistic outcomes. When you find yourself imagining the worst, pause and consider more likely, positive outcomes based on your skills and past experiences.

4. **Challenge perfectionism**: Set clear criteria for what 'good enough' looks like for each task. Remind yourself that perfection is often unattainable and can lead to diminishing returns.

5. **Regularly review and adjust your approach**: Stay mindful of the Dunning-Kruger effect by regularly reviewing the progress of your

work. Be open to adjusting your approach as you gain more insight into a task's complexity.

6. **Evaluate time and resources**: To combat the sunk-cost fallacy, regularly evaluate ongoing projects and tasks. Ask yourself, "Is continuing this path the most effective use of my time and resources?" Consult with colleagues to get a more subjective point of view.

7. **Create short-term rewards for long-term goals**: Mitigate present bias by setting up short-term rewards. This can provide the immediate gratification needed to stay on track with longer projects.

8. **Seek feedback**: Sometimes, an external perspective can help identify biases in your approach. Regularly seek feedback from colleagues or mentors to gain a different viewpoint on your work processes.

∼

DISTRACTIONS: THE GATEWAY TO PROCRASTINATION

The traditional boundaries between professional and personal life have become increasingly blurred, leading to a complex interplay of work-life interruptions. This phenomenon, often referred to as the Work-Life Boundary Theory, highlights the challenges in maintaining a clear separation between job responsibilities and personal life. Historically, the intrusion of work into personal time and vice versa has been a balancing act for many professionals. In an office setting, it's not uncommon for personal life to occasionally interrupt – a call from home, a WhatsApp message, or a quick online errand.

Conversely, at home, work often finds a way to creep in, whether it's responding to an after-hours email or finishing up a presentation. With the shift to remote work, these interruptions have become more entangled and frequent, leading to a scenario where the distinction between 'work time' and 'life time' is more ambiguous than ever. Navigating this requires not only discipline but also a strategic approach to minimise distractions and maintain focus, ensuring that neither sphere unduly encroaches upon the other.

Working from home often brings an unexpected guest into our professional lives: the array of distractions present in our home environments. For some, it might be the lure of household chores that suddenly seem appealing when faced with a challenging work task. For others, it could be the constant interruptions from family members or pets. Then there's the ever-present temptation of digital distractions – the siren call of social media, news websites, or the urge to constantly check emails.

The distraction log

Recognising the emergence of distractions involves a combination of self-awareness and honest assessment. In order to boost both of these, you could set up a distraction log.

Over the course of a week, jot down what distracts you and how often it occurs. For instance, you might notice that your focus wavers mid-morning, coinciding with the time you usually check social media. Or you might find out that interruptions are more frequent when you work in a certain part of the house.

Once you've identified your primary distractions, the next step is to find ways to mitigate them. This might mean setting specific times for checking social media or personal emails, so they don't intrude on work hours. For family interruptions, it could involve setting clear boundaries with household members, such as a 'do not disturb' sign or agreed-upon quiet hours. If noise is a distraction, noise-canceling headphones might be a worthwhile investment. The key is to create strategies tailored to your specific distractions and work habits.

The parking lot

Sometimes our distractions come from within, especially if we're struggling with a task. These inner distractions provide a great escape mechanism. Have you ever had a wonderful new idea for a new project when you were struggling to get half way through a current one? Or have you ever been about to start writing a difficult urgent email, when you've decided instead to start a report, even though it wasn't due for another week?

These thoughts will always pop up, but you can let go of them by writing them down in your calendar, or in your "parking lot" - an easy to access online space (or piece of paper) where you can write down important thoughts to come to later.

 "Procrastination is the thief of time, collar him." – Charles Dickens

MULTITASKING AS A PROCRASTINATION TACTIC

Meet Sarah, a remote worker who prides herself on being hyper-efficient at work. One fine morning, she sets out to conquer her workday: responding to emails while on a conference call, preparing a presentation during her team's brainstorming session, and simultaneously drafting a report while catching up on industry news. It's the multitasking ballet at its finest.

By noon, Sarah's day turns into a comedic symphony of chaos. The presentation looks more like an abstract art piece, her report reads like a cryptic puzzle, and let's not even talk about the email where she accidentally signed off with 'Love you, Mom'.

Sarah's day might sound like a scene from a sitcom, but it's a real-world reflection of a common misconception: that we can all multitask. In reality, our brains aren't wired to handle multiple complex tasks at the same time. Each switch between tasks can cause a cognitive reset, like a glitch in Sarah's multitasking matrix, leading to errors and reduced productivity. It's a classic case of doing more but accomplishing less.

When we think we're multitasking, we're actually just switching rapidly between tasks. Each switch might only take a fraction of a second, but it adds up, increasing the total time needed to complete the tasks by as much as 40%. It's like trying to cook dinner, watch a TV show, and knit a sweater at the same time – you might end up burning the dinner, missing the plot, and entangling the yarn.

A study from Stamford University in 2009 found that frequent multitaskers were more easily distracted and less able to maintain attention on a single task compared to those who multitasked less often. It turns out that multitasking, especially with electronic media, can lead to poorer cognitive control and reduced ability to focus on important tasks. The researchers found that heavy multitaskers were less efficient at organising their thoughts and filtering out irrelevant information, and they were slower at switching between tasks.

This becomes particularly relevant in remote work environments, where a computer is often the central tool for work. The temptation to juggle multiple tasks increases by the ease of switching between different applications and browser tabs. Each open window not only represents a distinct task but also adds to the cognitive load. Urgent emails, complex spreadsheets, and pending articles all compete for attention, each demanding a slice of your cognitive resources.

This form of multitasking closely resembles procrastination. While it may appear as a productive effort to tackle multiple tasks, it often results in shifting focus to less challenging or more immediately gratifying activities. Consequently, more critical or demanding tasks are delayed, which require undivided attention.

If you know that multitasking negatively affects your work, start by consciously prioritising your tasks. Each day, identify and list your most important tasks based on their urgency and relevance (for more on this, check out the Eisenhower Matrix in Chapter 6). Once you're in front of your computer, focus on creating a distraction-free environment by closing unnecessary applications and browser tabs. Finally, shift your mindset: rather than viewing multitasking as a productive skill, recognise it as a potential obstacle to deep work and meaningful productivity.

REMOTE WORK IS NOT JUST "WORKING FROM HOME"

Although remote work is often associated with working from home, some remote workers prefer to work from 'third spaces'—places other than the office or home. The most favoured among these are coworking spaces and cafés, and working from these can help combat procrastination.

For a start, when you or your company invest in a membership at a coworking space, there's an added motivation to make every minute count. In addition to that, coworking spaces are designed to provide a productive atmosphere. These environments often mimic an office setting, providing structured surroundings that can instil a sense of discipline and routine, and the presence of other professionals can also create a motivating atmosphere. However, it's important to choose a coworking space that aligns with your work style. For example, if you need quiet for concentration, a space with designated quiet areas would be ideal.

Working from cafés can offer a change of scenery and a dynamic environment that can stimulate creativity and productivity. The ambient noise and activity in a café can create a pleasant background that, for some people, enhances focus. Cafés can also be a good option for tasks that require less concentration or for brainstorming sessions. When working in cafés, time management techniques like the Pomodoro Technique (of which more in Chapter 6) can be particularly useful, as they encourage working in focused bursts, suitable for the sometimes unpredictable café environment.

In both coworking spaces and cafés, the strategies to combat procrastination remain similar to those in a home setting. Breaking tasks into smaller steps, setting specific goals, and minimising distractions are universally applicable. However, the social aspect of these spaces can be leveraged to your advantage. For instance, in a coworking space, having an accountability partner or participating in productivity-focused events can enhance motivation. In cafés, the limited time you might spend there (perhaps as long as your coffee lasts) can be used as a natural time-boxing tool to focus on specific tasks.

SHORT-TERM TACTICS TO COMBAT PROCRASTINATION

The essence of overcoming procrastination lies in recognising the barriers holding you back. While there's no instant quick fix, the previous sections of this chapter should have equipped you with valuable insights. As you continue to develop your self-awareness, consider these practical tactics for immediate application to help combat procrastination.

1. **Break down large tasks**

Procrastination often strikes when a task appears too daunting. Breaking down large projects into smaller, manageable steps can make them seem less intimidating. For instance, if you have to write a report, start by outlining the sections, then focus on writing one section at a time.

2. **Minimise distractions**

Identify what commonly distracts you (social media, household chores, etc.) and take steps to minimise these distractions during work hours. This might mean using website blockers or setting a specific time for chores.

3. **Implement a reward system**

Reward yourself for completing tasks. For example, after finishing a challenging task, you might treat yourself to a coffee break, a short walk, or an episode of your favourite show.

4. Practice mindfulness and self-compassion

Be aware of when you start procrastinating and gently guide yourself back to the task without self-criticism. Mindfulness can help you stay focused on the present task and reduce anxiety about future tasks.

5. Accountability partners

Pairing up with a colleague or friend to share progress can increase your sense of responsibility and motivation. Regular check-ins can provide both support and a gentle nudge to stay on track.

6. Reflect and adjust

At the end of each day or week, reflect on what you accomplished and what led to procrastination. Understanding your patterns can help you adjust your strategies to be more effective.

7. Create a dedicated workspace

Having a specific area in your home designated for work can create a mental distinction between 'work time' and 'personal time', helping to reduce the temptation to engage in non-work-related activities.

QUICK CONTENT SUMMARY

- Defining procrastination and its impact on productivity.
- Identifying and addressing cognitive biases like catastrophising and optimism bias.
- Practical steps to recognise and counteract procrastination tendencies.
- Quick-fix strategies to overcome procrastination in the short term.

PRODUCTIVITY PATHFINDERS

1. Identify Your Procrastination Triggers: Take note of when and why you tend to procrastinate. Is it a particular type of task, time of day, or feeling of overwhelm?
2. Challenge Cognitive Biases: When you catch yourself catastrophising or falling for the optimism bias, pause and reassess the situation with a more balanced perspective.
3. Create a Distraction-Free Environment: Identify the external distractions in your home or chosen work environment and take proactive steps to minimise them.
4. Start a Distraction Journal: identify the triggers for your internal and external distractions and create strategies to reduce them.

CHAPTER 3
SEPARATING WORK FROM "LIFE" - OR NOT

This chapter explores the varied approaches to balancing—or blending—professional and personal spheres. We challenge the traditional notion of Work-Life Balance and introduce alternative perspectives that may resonate more closely with contemporary working styles.

We will also examine the identities of 'separators' and 'integrators'—those who prefer clear boundaries versus those who favour a more blended experience. Understanding your inclination can inform how you structure your work environment, manage your time, and interact with others who may have different preferences.

This chapter is not just about understanding different work-life philosophies but also about identifying your own preferences and learning how to communicate and collaborate with others who may view the work-life equation differently. By recognising and respecting these differences, we can foster a more supportive and productive remote work culture.

SEPARATORS AND INTEGRATORS

If life were simple, we could all fit under one of the 'work-life' boxes, explain to people how we operate, and live in work-harmony together. However, often we find ourselves working with people who see the work-life relationship differently to us. This can impact our collaboration, especially if we have different schedules to our colleagues.

How you see your work fitting into your life will impact your day to day, and the boundaries you place around your work. For the sake of simplicity, let's have a look at two terms that describe different approaches individuals take to manage the boundaries between their work and personal lives.

Separators

Separators are individuals who prefer a clear and distinct boundary between their work and personal life. They thrive on compartmentalisation, keeping their professional and personal roles and responsibilities separate. For separators, this distinction is crucial for mental well-being and productivity.

A separator might be someone like Jenna, who designates a specific room in her house as her office. When she's in this space, it's all about work. At the end of her workday, she physically leaves the room and closes the door behind her, signalling a shift from her professional to personal life. Jenna avoids checking work emails or taking business calls once she's outside her home office. For her, these physical and digital boundaries are essential to switch off from work mode and engage fully with her personal life.

Integrators

On the other hand, Carlos is a stay-at-home dad, whose approach is to integrate his work and parenting roles throughout the day. He might answer emails while having breakfast with his children or take a work call during a mid-morning break. Carlos finds that this integrated approach allows him to be productive in his work while being present for his family.

He is an integrator. Integrators are more fluid in how they transition between work and personal tasks and often find that intertwining these aspects of their lives is more natural and less stressful.

Clash of titans

Understanding whether you are a separator or an integrator can significantly influence how you structure your work life. For separators, creating a dedicated workspace, setting strict work hours, and using different devices for work and personal use can be effective strategies. Separators benefit from clear rituals that mark the beginning and end of the workday, like changing into work attire even when working from home or having a specific end-of-day routine.

Integrators, however, might prefer a more flexible schedule. They may work in different areas of their home and might not mind the intermingling of work and personal tasks. Integrators often need to be more vigilant about ensuring that work doesn't completely overtake personal time, as their fluid boundaries can sometimes lead to longer work hours.

Both approaches have their merits and challenges, and the suitability of each depends on individual preferences, work requirements, and personal circumstances. When working remotely, when you tend to have some degree of autonomy to design your workday, understanding your natural inclination towards separation or integration can help in creating a work environment that suits your style.

When separators and integrators collaborate in a remote work environment, the intersection of their distinct work styles can present unique challenges.

For a separator, such as Jenna, who thrives on clear boundaries between work and personal life, working with an integrator like Carlos can be challenging. Jenna prefers to schedule meetings within her designated work hours and is meticulous about not letting work spill into her personal time. On the other hand, Carlos, comfortable with blending his work and personal activities, might send work-related messages or emails outside of traditional work hours. This difference in approach can lead to misunderstandings or frustration. Jenna might feel pressured to respond to Carlos' late-night emails, while Carlos might perceive Jenna's adherence to strict work hours as inflexibility.

The key to making this collaboration work is mutual respect and communication. Through discussing and acknowledging different working styles integrators and separators can establish clear expectations and boundaries. For instance, Jenna and Carlos could agree on a compromise where Carlos is mindful not to expect immediate responses to communications outside of Jenna's working hours, while Jenna tries to accommodate occasional urgent requests that fall outside her normal schedule.

Quiz: Are You a Separator, Integrator, or a Blend?

To reflect on how you approach your "work" and "life", you can start with a quick self-awareness quiz, which can tell you whether you are likely a separator or an integrator. If you have team members you work with, taking the survey individually and sharing the results collectively can generate some fruitful discussions, and help you to agree on how to work together.

For each question, choose the option that best resonates with you. Keep track of your answers, but don't worry about the points yet. You'll calculate your score at the end.

1. Managing work email outside official work hours:

- A. Check and respond only if urgent.

- B. Respond immediately.

- C. Wait to respond during work hours.

2. Preferred location for working at home:
- A. In a designated work area.
- B. Mostly in my workspace, but sometimes elsewhere.
- C. Anywhere, I like changing spots.

3. Routine for unwinding after work:
- A. Specific routine to disconnect.
- B. No particular routine.
- C. Sometimes follow a routine.

4. Handling personal tasks during work hours:
- A. Rarely, I keep them separate.
- B. As they come, along with work tasks.
- C. Usually separate, but occasionally mix.

5. Taking work calls on a day off:
- A. Only if it's an emergency.
- B. Prefer not to, but will if important.
- C. I'm fine with it, it's part of the job.

6. Organisation of your workspace:
- A. Strictly for work.

- B. A mix of work and personal items.

- C. Mainly for work, with some personal items.

7. Strategy for prioritising tasks:

- A. Work tasks during work hours, personal afterward.

- B. Based on urgency, work or personal.

- C. Generally separate but flexible based on urgency.

8. Responding to personal matters during the workday:

- A. Reschedule and refocus on work.

- B. Adjust work around them.

- C. Handle them but return to work soon.

Scoring

Question 1: A=2, B=3, C=1

Question 2: A=1, B=2, C=3

Question 3: A=1, B=3, C=2

Question 4: A=1, B=3, C=2

Question 5: A=1, B=2, C=3

Question 6: A=1, B=3, C=2

Question 7: A=1, B=3, C=2

Question 8: A=2, B=3, C=1

- 8-12 Points: You are a Separator. You prefer clear distinctions between work and personal life.

- 13-21 Points: You are a Blend. You balance separation and integration, adapting as needed.

- 22-24 Points: You are an Integrator. You comfortably mix work and personal life without strict boundaries.

Remember that this quiz is not a formal or academic assessment. It's designed to offer a moment of reflection on your own work style preferences and habits.

Additionally, this quiz can serve as an interesting conversation starter with colleagues. Discussing your results with others may provide insights into different work-life balance approaches and foster a supportive work environment where diverse work styles are acknowledged and respected.

WORK-LIFE DYNAMICS

We often hear how important it is to achieve Work-Life Balance. This concept gained prominence in the 1970s and 1980s, as more dual-income households emerged and the challenges of balancing work and family life became a more prominent societal issue. This is the most traditional term associated with making sure that work doesn't take over our whole day, at the expense of not having any personal time left over for family, friends and other valuable things besides work. It's about equally prioritising the demands of one's career and the demands of one's personal life.

If you find yourself striving for an equal distribution of time and energy between work and personal life, the traditional concept of Work-Life Balance may appeal to you (and you might have scored highly as a "separator" in the previous test). This approach is about drawing clear boundaries, where work and personal life are distinct and given equal priority. It suits those who thrive on compartmentalisation and need a clear separation to function effectively in both areas.

However, not everybody aims to achieve Work-Life Balance, and indeed, some people don't like to refer to "work" as something that's in opposition to "life". Here are other terms that have gained popularity as work has taken over a higher profile in discussions about wellbeing.

Work-Life Integration

Unlike Work-Life Balance, which suggests a strict separation between work and personal life, work-life integration is about blending them together. It recognises that work and life are not necessarily in opposition and can be integrated in a way that benefits both areas. This term gained traction at the beginning of this century, reflecting changes in technology and work practices that have made the clear boundaries of work and personal life more permeable. It's a concept that has been discussed by various thought leaders in the field of human resources and organisational psychology, especially in the context of the increasing flexibility of work facilitated by digital technology.

If your work and personal life are deeply intertwined, you might lean towards Work-Life Integration. This approach is less about balancing two separate spheres and more about finding synergy between them. It acknowledges that work and life often intermingle and seeks to create a holistic lifestyle where one complements the other.

Work-Life Fit

This term acknowledges that the 'best fit' between work and personal life can vary greatly from person to person and over time. It's about finding a personalised balance that works for the individual's current life situation. The concept of Work-Life Fit has been prominently advocated by Cali Williams Yost, a flexible workplace strategist and author. Yost's perspective is that 'fit' is a more realistic and individualised way of thinking about how work and personal life can complement each other.

For those who believe that the ideal balance is unique and ever-changing, Work-Life Fit might resonate more. This approach is highly individualistic, recognising that the 'perfect balance' can vary greatly from person to person and even from one life stage to another. It emphasises creating a personalised approach to managing work and life responsibilities.

Work-Life Negotiation

Are you constantly fine-tuning the balance between your professional and personal life? If so, the concept of Work-Life Negotiation might speak to you. Unlike static models of work-life balance, Work-Life Negotiation acknowledges that our priorities and commitments are always in flux. It's a recognition that balancing work and life is not a one-time setup but an ongoing process of adjustment.

This concept is particularly suited for those who embrace flexibility and understand that life's demands can shift unexpectedly. Here, the focus is on the art of skilfully navigating these changes, constantly negotiating where and how to spend your time and energy. Work-Life Negotiation is about finding a balance that's not just sustainable, but also responsive to the evolving chapters of your professional and personal life.

 "You will never feel truly satisfied by work until you are satisfied by life." – Heather Schuck

YOUR "WORK-LIFE" RELATIONSHIP

Spend some time thinking about which of these concepts resonates most with you.

In determining which of these concepts aligns with your needs, remember that the choice is deeply personal and should be dictated by your own preferences, lifestyle, and goals. It's important not to let external pressures or popular trends dictate the kind of balance you strive for. Whatever approach you choose should support a lifestyle that sustains your well-being, keeps you productive and fulfilled, and allows you to thrive in both your professional and personal life.

Here are five questions to help you identify the concept that aligns best with your preferences and lifestyle. You might want to come back to them in six or twelve months, as your answers might change as time goes by.

1. How do you react to the blending of work and personal life?

Reflect on how you feel when your work and personal life intermingle. Are you comfortable with a fluid blend of the two, or do you prefer keeping them distinctly separate?

2. What does your ideal day look like?

Imagine your perfect workday. Does it involve strict boundaries between work and personal activities, or do you envision integrating personal tasks and work responsibilities throughout the day?

3. How do you define success in your personal and professional life?

Consider what success means to you in both areas. Is it about achieving a perfect balance, or is it more about how seamlessly these parts of your life complement and enrich each other?

4. How comfortable are you with flexibility and change?

Assess your comfort level with flexibility in your schedule. Do you thrive in a dynamic environment where work and life responsibilities are constantly negotiated, or do you prefer a more stable and predictable division?

5. What are your priorities and how do they influence your daily life?

Think about your current priorities in life and work. Are your personal and professional goals intertwined, or do they require distinct and separate focus and energy?

Gaining clarity on the role you want work to play in your life can help you plan your time and identify your priorities.

QUICK CONTENT SUMMARY

- Concepts of work-life balance, integration, fit and negotiation.
- Characteristics and strategies for separators and integrators.
- Balancing collaboration and personal work styles in remote settings.

PRODUCTIVITY PATHFINDERS

1. Define Your Work-Life Preference: Take a moment to really think about whether you prefer work-life balance, integration, or fit. Write down which concept resonates with you and why. (Or maybe you'd like to come up with your own term.)
2. Assess Your Environment: Look at your current working environment through the lens of your work-life preference. What changes can you make to better support your chosen strategy?
3. Reflect on Your Interactions with Colleagues: After collaborating with others, reflect on whether your work-life preference is complementary or conflicting with theirs, and think of ways to improve the dynamic.

CHAPTER 4
YOUR PHYSICAL ENVIRONMENT AND RESOURCES

Chapter 4 is dedicated to the impact your physical workspace and the resources within it have on productivity, well-being, and overall job satisfaction. The shift to remote work has brought to the forefront the importance of designing a personal workspace that is not only functional but also conducive to our well-being. While this chapter will focus primarily on optimising the home environment, the principles discussed can be applied to other remote working scenarios, like cafés and coworking spaces.

As you read through this chapter, reflect on how your environment and the tools you use fit into the larger picture of your work-life dynamic. The ultimate goal is to forge a space that not only serves your professional needs but also supports your personal satisfaction and efficiency.

CRAFTING YOUR IDEAL WORKSPACE

Let's dive straight away into designing the ideal work spot: a harmonious blend of practicality and comfort, with minimum external distractions.

1) **Location**

When choosing a spot to work from at home, consider finding a space with natural lighting; a space with plenty of daylight can boost your mood and energy levels, reducing eye strain and fatigue. Ensure that your screen is placed to avoid glare, which can strain your eyes over time. Additionally, consider the lighting for video calls; ideally, windows should not be directly behind you to prevent backlighting, which can make it difficult for others to see you clearly.

On the other hand, some people might prefer a 'black box' style space, for enhanced focus and minimal distractions. If that's the case, make sure that you take regular breaks, and leave the room regularly to absorb some natural light.

2) **Noise levels**

A room away from the hustle and bustle of household activities, like a spare bedroom or a quiet corner in your living space, can provide the tranquility necessary for concentration. Also, consider the flow of foot traffic. Setting up your office in a high-traffic area might seem convenient but can lead to frequent interruptions.

Once again, this set up might not suit everyone. I know plenty of people who cannot concentrate in places where it's so quiet you can hear a pin drop.

3) **Your chair and desk**

The cornerstone of any home office is a good chair. Investing in an ergonomically designed chair can make a world of difference, providing the necessary support to prevent back pain and discomfort during long working hours. Similarly, the height and setup of your desk are crucial. Your desk should be at a height that allows your arms to rest comfortably at a 90-degree angle, reducing strain on your shoulders and wrists.

4) Ergonomics

Your keyboard should be easily reachable and at a comfortable height. Consider using a keyboard tray if your desk height is not adjustable. An ergonomic setup is not just about comfort; it directly impacts your productivity and health, reducing the risk of repetitive strain injuries and maintaining your energy levels throughout the day.

An ergonomic setup impacts your productivity and health.

PERSONALISING YOUR SPACE

Personalising your workspace is like adding seasoning to a dish – it enhances the flavour and makes it uniquely yours. But just as with cooking, there's an art to finding the right balance. Your home office is not just a reflection of your professional life but also a personal space that should inspire and motivate you. Imagine your workspace as a canvas where functionality meets your personal style. It could be as simple as choosing a colour scheme that calms or energises you, or as elaborate as displaying an eclectic collection of items that spark creativity – think of a wall adorned with inspiring quotes, a shelf of your favourite books, or a cherished photo that reminds you of your goals. These personal touches can transform a sterile office into a welcoming and inspiring environment, making the start of your workday something to look forward to.

While personalisation is important, it's essential to strike a balance with professional functionality. An over-cluttered desk with too many personal items can become a distraction rather than a source of inspiration. The key is to integrate personal elements in a way that complements, rather than competes with, your work. For instance, you might choose ergonomic accessories that match your personal style, or organise your desk with stylish yet functional items. Think of it as creating a harmonious symphony where each element – from your comfortable, ergonomically designed chair to the art on the walls – plays a part in fostering both productivity and personal well-being. It's about creating a space that not only serves your professional needs but also resonates with your personal identity.

Choosing your work space away from home

If you prefer to work from a coworking space or café, it's worth spending some time thinking about what environment will help you do your best work. Choosing the right café or coworking space is as important as setting up an efficient home office, especially if you thrive in a more dynamic environment or seek occasional changes in your work setting.

When selecting a café, consider factors like the availability of power outlets, Wi-Fi strength, and the general ambiance. A café with a steady hum of background noise can be invigorating for some, but distracting for others. The ideal café is one where the atmosphere aligns with your work style – lively enough to keep you energised but not so hectic that it disrupts your concentration. Additionally, look for cafés that are comfortable with patrons working for extended periods and have ample seating to avoid the mid-day rush hour scramble for a spot - and look out for any posted signs indicating restrictions on laptop use, whether during specific hours or altogether.

In the case of coworking spaces, the considerations are more nuanced. Start by evaluating the location – it should be conveniently accessible, reducing the time and stress of commuting. Assess the amenities offered: does the space have private meeting rooms, phone booths for confidential calls, or communal areas for serendipitous encounters?

The layout of the coworking space will also affect your productivity. Open-plan spaces can be great for collaboration and networking, but if your work requires quiet and concentration, look for a coworking space that offers private desks or quiet zones.

Lastly, pay attention to the community and culture of the coworking space. The best coworking spaces foster a community that aligns with your professional values and work style, offering networking opportunities and potential collaborations.

Whether choosing a café or a coworking space, the key is to find environments that not only provide the practical tools and amenities needed for effective work but also complement and enhance your working style and well-being. These external workspaces can offer valuable alternatives to the home office, providing variety and balance to your remote working experience.

"Environment is the invisible hand that shapes human behaviour." – James Clear

A SPOT FIT FOR MEETINGS

Love them or hate them, online meetings have become a part of every remote worker's week. For those working from home, video calls have become a window into our personal spaces, blending the professional with the personal. This dual nature of video conferencing brings an additional layer to consider in your home office design, or your choice of external space.

When engaging in casual team meetings, a more personalised backdrop can serve as a conversation starter, offering a glimpse of your personality and interests. It's an opportunity to build rapport with colleagues, where a well-placed piece of artwork or an interesting bookshelf can add warmth to the digital interaction. However, the story changes slightly when the call involves clients or external members of the organisation, especially those you don't know well. In such cases, it's prudent to maintain a balance that leans more towards professionalism. This doesn't mean stripping away all personal elements, but rather curating your visible workspace to project a professional image. For instance, you might reposition your camera to focus on a more neutral background or ensure that personal items in view are tidy and not overly distracting. The goal is to create a backdrop that is both professional and comfortable, one that suits the tone of the meeting without losing the essence of your personal workspace.

An alternative solution for managing the backdrop of video calls is to use virtual backgrounds within your meeting tool. This offers a hassle-free alternative to constantly adjusting your physical space, particularly for those without a dedicated office or working in multi-purpose areas. Virtual backgrounds can instantly provide a professional or neutral setting, irrespective of your actual surroundings, and can range from a sleek, minimalist office look to creative or branded backdrops that align with your organisation's aesthetic. However, it's important to be mindful of lighting and contrasting colours, as poor lighting or colours that blend with the virtual background can lead to visual issues like fading or objects appearing and disappearing. Moreover, these backgrounds can be quickly switched, ensuring flexibility and preparedness for any type of meeting.

ESSENTIAL TOOLS AND TECHNOLOGY FOR REMOTE WORK

As well as having a suitable physical space, as a remote worker you need to have access to suitable equipment and technology.

Reliable internet connection

The backbone of successful remote work is a reliable internet connection. Understanding your bandwidth needs is critical, as tasks such as video conferencing, cloud-based services, and large file transfers require a stable and fast internet connection. It's worthwhile to invest in a high-quality router and consider a backup option like a mobile hotspot for emergencies. Whenever possible, connect your computer directly to the internet using a cable for a more stable connection. You should also regularly test your internet speed and upgrade your plans if necessary to meet your work requirements.

Hardware essentials

In terms of hardware, freelancers typically face limitations based on their budget, whereas employed remote workers often rely on equipment provided by their employers. However, not all companies offer the same level of equipment. In some cases, employees may have to use their personal devices, which can vary in quality and suitability for work tasks. A good quality computer that can handle multiple applications simultaneously is now a given. Additionally, peripherals like a comfortable keyboard, an ergonomic mouse, and possibly a secondary monitor can significantly enhance productivity.

Many companies have stipends or reimbursement policies for remote workers to purchase or upgrade their home office equipment. This not only helps in ensuring that employees have the necessary tools but also shows the company's commitment to supporting their staff in remote settings.

Software and applications

When it comes to software, you might not always have the freedom to install your preferred applications due to company policies or security reasons. Many organisations require employees to seek permission before adding any software to their work computers to maintain security protocols. However, common tools often approved include communication software like Slack and Zoom, and the ever popular Office 365 (which includes Microsoft Teams).

Backup and security

Some companies, especially those with stringent IT policies, may provide pre-approved software suites that employees are required to use. Whether you work for an organisation or yourself, make sure that your devices are protected with updated antivirus software, and that you are aware of security protocols: use strong passwords and be vigilant about phishing attacks. In some regions, companies provide cybersecurity training to equip their employees with the knowledge to protect themselves and the company from cyber threats.

Make sure you're regularly backing up your work, in case of hardware failure, accidental deletion, or cyber threats. A lot of your work might be stored and accessed in the cloud, but you might be using specialist applications or have private documents you prefer to keep on your own device. (Before you ask what any of this has to do with time management, think of all the time you'll waste if your work gets lost or corrupted.)

The balance between company policy and employee needs

While some employees are fortunate to work for organisations that provide flexibility and a budget for setting up an optimal home office, others may need to adapt to less-than-ideal tech setups. Know where the limits are, and keep checking in with HQ, as policies and app availability often change. If you work for yourself or for an organisation that prefers you to 'bring your own device', or allows teams to take ownership of their tool stack, make sure you continuously revisit your subscriptions, and evaluate whether the tool is helping you do your best work, or whether your work has ended up adapting to the tool.

QUICK CONTENT SUMMARY

- Tips for setting up an effective home office.
- Choosing the right environment in coworking spaces and cafés.
- Overview of essential hardware and software for remote work.

PRODUCTIVITY PATHFINDERS

1. Evaluate Your Current Workspace: Take a critical look at your current work environment at home. What aspects work well for you, and what could be improved?
2. Personalise with Purpose: Add personal touches to your workspace that inspire and motivate you, but be careful not to clutter your space. Aim for a balance between personalisation and functionality.
3. Prepare for Part 2: In Part 2 we'll dive into actionable advice on planning your day, prioritising tasks, and setting boundaries—key components of effective time management. Reflect on how the design of your physical workspace will support the time management and productivity strategies you'll learn in Part 2. Consider what adjustments you might need to make to maximise the benefits of the upcoming advice.

PART 2: TACTICS AND STRATEGIES

CHAPTER 5
PLANNING AND REVIEWING ROUTINES

Chapter 5 marks the beginning of Part 2, where we shift from establishing the fundamentals of remote work to implementing practical strategies for daily and weekly planning.

We'll explore how the first hours after you wake—your 'morning', irrespective of the actual time—can influence the trajectory of your entire day, we'll introduce the concept of the 'Not To-Do List', and advocate for the practice of regular reflection and planning, from daily reviews to a comprehensive weekly recap.

CRAFTING THE FIRST HOURS OF YOUR DAY

> "Those who every morning plan the transactions of the day and follow out that plan carry a thread that will guide them through the labyrinth of the most busy life."
> – Victor Hugo

Adopting a morning routine, no matter what time your day starts, can set a positive tone for the rest of your day. The term 'morning' here is flexible; it refers to the first few hours after you wake up, whether that's at the crack of dawn or closer to noon. For early risers, the tranquility of dawn offers a serene backdrop for focused work or contemplation. For those who are more alert and energetic later in the day, their 'morning' routine might kick off mid-morning or even in the afternoon. The key is to harness the first hours of your waking day, whenever they occur.

A morning routine should be personally tailored to suit individual lifestyles and work requirements. It could involve physical exercise, which not only invigorates the body but also clears the mind, setting a proactive tone for the day. Meditation or even a simple practice of gratitude can centre the mind, allowing for a calm yet focused start. For some, engaging in a creative hobby or reading can stimulate the brain and help you start the day with a smile. The goal of these activities is to transition into your workday with a sense of preparedness and mental clarity.

The calm and quiet of the morning provide an environment conducive to creative brainstorming. This could involve exploring new project ideas, thinking through innovative solutions to complex problems, or simply engaging in free-form creative activities like sketching or writing.

Similarly, the early hours can be strategically used for long-term planning and big-picture thinking. With a clear mind, you can effectively map out long-term projects, set goals, and contemplate strategic directions without the pressure of immediate deadlines or ongoing tasks. This time can be used to reflect on broader business objectives, analyse market trends, or plan professional growth paths. It's about utilising the tranquility of the morning to focus on where you want to go, both in your current projects and in your career trajectory.

There is not one way to start your day. Understanding and respecting your internal clock and knowing the type of activities that help you kick off your day with energy is not just a matter of personal preference; it's a strategic approach to maximise your effectiveness and efficiency in those first hours of your day.

FINDING CLARITY AND CREATIVITY THROUGH FREE WRITING

Some knowledge workers like to start their day by 'checking in' with themselves on paper. This can be done following Julia Cameron's Morning Pages, a practice popular with writers and other artists.

Morning Pages involve writing three pages of longhand, stream-of-consciousness writing, done first thing in the morning. This practice, originally intended for artists to unlock their creativity and overcome mental blocks, can also be beneficial for remote workers in various ways.

Clearing the mind

Just as Morning Pages allow artists to spill out their thoughts and fears, you can use this tool to clear your mind of any lingering anxieties, doubts, or distractions. Writing down worries or tasks that are occupying your mind can create mental clarity and focus, which is especially important in a remote working environment where self-direction plays an important role.

Sparking creativity

If your job involves creative thinking or problem-solving, Morning Pages can serve as a catalyst for creativity. The unstructured, free-flow nature of the writing encourages the flow of ideas and can often lead to unexpected solutions or innovative approaches to work-related challenges.

Planning and reflection

While traditionally not meant for planning, you can adapt Morning Pages to include a brief section for setting daily goals or intentions. This practice can help in structuring the day ahead, especially for those who struggle with self-organisation. It's also a space for reflective thinking, which can be valuable for personal and professional growth. Think of it as a water cooler moment with your page.

To integrate Morning Pages into your routine, you don't need to strictly adhere to the three-page rule or even the morning timing. The essence lies in regular, unfiltered writing, which can be adjusted to your schedule and preferences.

"Reviewing what you have learned and learning anew, you are fit to be a teacher." – Confucius

THE UNSUNG HERO OF PRODUCTIVITY: THE 'NOT TO-DO LIST'

This list is where good intentions go to get a reality check.

It's like the anti-bucket list for your daily life, full of activities that you've wisely decided are a no-go.

Imagine jotting down: "Do not start the day scrolling through social media," followed by, "Avoid organising the spice rack during work hours," and the classic, "Resist the urge to binge-watch a new series at lunch." These entries are not just reminders; they're little victories against the artful dodge of procrastination.

The Not To-Do List can be surprisingly liberating. It's like telling yourself all the things you don't have to worry about. And there's a strange joy in checking off something by not doing it. "Didn't reorganise my entire bookshelf alphabetically instead of finishing the report? Check!"

In the grand drama of knowledge work, where distractions wear the villain's mask, the Not To-Do List is the superhero we didn't know we needed. So, go ahead and list down those tempting but ultimately unproductive tasks. By acknowledging what you shouldn't do, you might just find more time for the things you really should be doing – or at least, you'll have a good chuckle in the process.

ENDING YOUR DAY

The absence of a physical commute that traditionally signals the end of a workday means that those working from home need to establish their own routines to transition from work mode to personal time.

The concept of an evening routine is often overshadowed by the emphasis on how we start our day. An evening routine is not just about marking the end of the workday; it's a ritual that helps in transitioning from professional responsibilities to personal time. These rituals could be as simple as shutting down your computer, closing the door to your home office, or even a symbolic gesture like turning off a specific desk lamp.

The following types of rituals can help in mentally disengaging from work tasks and shifting your focus towards personal time.

Preparing for the next day

Spend a few minutes planning your tasks for the next day. This not only helps in easing anxiety about upcoming work but also ensures that you can enjoy your evening without work-related thoughts lingering in the back of your mind.

Engaging in physical activities

A short walk outside (your 'commute' back home), a yoga/Pilates session, or even light stretching can help to clear your mind and relieve any tension built up from sitting at a desk all day. These activities not only mark the end of your workday but also serve as a physical signal to your body that it's time to relax and recharge.

Embracing stillness

If you need time to unwind both body and mind, you can set time for meditation for a few minutes at the end of your workday, or simply close your eyes and reflect on the day's achievements and challenges.

Recording your gratitude

Consider keeping a journal where you jot down all the things you achieved during the day, or that you are grateful for. This can be a simple way to end the day with a positive feeling.

However, you don't need a complete switch from 'work' to 'life' at the end of your day, if that's not what you want. You can integrate light professional development activities into your evening routine. This might include reading an industry-related article, watching a webinar, or even casual networking through professional social media platforms or events in your coworking space. The key here is to ensure that these activities are not stressful or too closely related to the day's work, so that you have plenty of time to disconnect before going to bed. Whatever you give time to at the end of the day should be about personal growth and interest rather than an extension of the workday.

A STRUCTURED END OF DAY ROUTINE

If you're navigating a particularly challenging period at work or undergoing significant changes, consider adopting a more structured approach to your unwinding routine. Here's a methodical framework you can follow.

1. Reflect on your day

Start by taking a few minutes to reflect on your day. What were the major tasks you accomplished? What challenges did you face and how did you address them? This reflection can be done through journaling or simply pondering over the day's events. (We'll look into journaling in more depth in Chapter 10.)

Consider what went well and why. Acknowledge your successes, no matter how small, and think about the factors that contributed to these successes. This positive reflection helps in building confidence and recognising your capabilities.

2. **Analyse challenges and lessons**

Identify any challenges or obstacles you encountered. What were the stumbling blocks? Was it a lack of resources, distractions, or perhaps a skill that needs improvement?

For each challenge, try to extract a lesson or an area for improvement.

3. **Plan for tomorrow**

Based on your reflection, start planning for the next day. Prioritise tasks that are most important or time-sensitive.

Consider the lessons learned from today's challenges and how you can apply them to tomorrow's tasks. For example, if you identified that a particular task took longer than expected, allocate more time for similar tasks in the future.

4. **Prepare a To-Do List**

Create a To-Do List for the next day. This list should not just be about work tasks but also include any personal activities or breaks to ensure a balanced day. Organise the list in a way that aligns with your energy levels throughout the day. For instance, if you're more focused in the morning, schedule demanding tasks during that time.

Alternatively, if you found yourself spending time in activities that brought you no joy or value, prepare a "Not-To-Do List" instead.

5. **Set up for a good start**

Lastly, prepare your workspace for the next day. This might mean tidying up your desk, setting out materials you'll need, or writing down key points to address first thing in the morning.

Consider also setting up a mental framework for the next day. Envision yourself successfully tackling the day's tasks, which can set a positive tone for when you start work.

∼

QUICK CONTENT SUMMARY

- Establishing a personalised morning routine.
- Aligning tasks with peak productivity times.
- The role of journaling for growth and reflection.
- Evening routines for transitioning from work mode to personal time.
- Conducting weekly reviews for continuous improvement.

∼

PRODUCTIVITY PATHFINDERS

1. Craft Your Personal Morning Routine: Reflect on what activities energise you and incorporate them into the first hours after you wake up. This could be exercise, reading, or 'Morning Pages'.
2. Establish Evening Wind-Down Rituals: Create a routine that helps you transition from work to personal time, such as a walk, a leisurely activity, or planning for the next day.
3. Tweak Your Routines as Needed: Be willing to adjust your morning and evening routines as you discover what works best for you.

CHAPTER 6
POPULAR TIME MANAGEMENT AND PLANNING TECHNIQUES

> "The bad news is time flies. The good news is you're the pilot." – Michael Altshuler

Chapter 6 is a collection of popular productivity methods. As you read through these techniques, remember that there is no one-size-fits-all solution. The best approach is the one that integrates smoothly into your life and helps you achieve your goals with less stress and more satisfaction.

THE EISENHOWER MATRIX

This model looks at prioritising your tasks by assessing their level of urgency and importance. The Eisenhower Matrix was named after US President Dwight D. Eisenhower, known for his exceptional time management skills and his ability to prioritise tasks effectively. The matrix was later popularised by Stephen Covey in the now classic book, "The 7 Habits of Highly Effective People."

The matrix divides tasks into four quadrants:

- Urgent and important
- Important but not urgent
- Urgent but not important
- Neither urgent nor important.

This technique can help you with decision-making about which tasks to focus on immediately (urgent and important), which to schedule for later (important but not urgent), which to delegate or request assistance with (not important but urgent), and which to eliminate altogether. The matrix can help you to focus on activities that align with your goals and contribute to your long-term success.

	URGENT	NOT URGENT
IMPORTANT	Do	Schedule
NOT IMPORTANT	Delegate (Ask!)	Forget

Use the matrix to plan your day and week.

In a dynamic environment, these categories are often fluid. For example, a task that was important but not urgent in the morning can become urgent by afternoon due to external factors. So don't forget to revisit your matrix before creating your next To-Do List!

THE POMODORO TECHNIQUE

The Pomodoro Technique was developed in the late 1980s by Francesco Cirillo, when he was studying at university in Italy.

Struggling with time management and maintaining concentration, Cirillo experimented with a simple idea: dividing his work into short, timed intervals to create a sense of urgency and focus. He used a kitchen timer shaped like a tomato (*pomodoro* in Italian) for these intervals, which is how the technique got its name.

Divide your work time into 'pomodoros'.

Cirillo discovered that by working in these short bursts (which he initially set at 25 minutes, followed by a short break), he could improve his concentration and productivity. The technique not only helped him manage his time more effectively but also kept his energy levels high throughout the day.

The Pomodoro Technique has since gained popularity as a simple yet effective time management method that helps individuals break their work into intervals, traditionally 25 minutes in length, separated by short breaks. This approach is particularly beneficial in managing attention and reducing the cognitive fatigue associated with long periods of focus. It is popular with writers, but you can use it for any kind of work.

THE 90-MINUTE WORK CYCLE FOR DEEP FOCUS

In contrast to the Pomodoro Technique, the 90-minute work cycle caters to those who thrive on longer periods of uninterrupted focus, allowing them to delve deeply into complex tasks and creative thought processes. It's recommended for tasks that require deep concentration, and is based on Tony Schwartz and Jim Loehr's book "The Power of Full Engagement."

Schwartz and Loehr's research in performance psychology reveals a pattern in human energy levels known as the 'ultradian rhythm'. This rhythm dictates that our bodies naturally cycle from a state of high energy to a state of physiological fatigue approximately every 90 minutes. By aligning our work patterns with this natural rhythm, we can optimise our productivity and focus.

The 90-minute work cycle technique encourages individuals to work in focused, uninterrupted sprints of around 90 minutes, followed by a brief period of rest or a less intense activity. This break could involve a physical activity, a short walk, a relaxation exercise, or simply stepping away from the work environment. The key is to allow for a full mental and physical recharge before diving into the next cycle of intense work.

When experimenting with the 90-minute work cycle, remember that everyone's capacity for sustained focus can vary. Some people may find that a slightly shorter or longer period of focused work is more effective for them. Others might discover that the nature of their work requires adjustments to the length of their focus sessions or breaks.

TIME BLOCKING AND TASK BATCHING

Time Blocking (as its name suggests) involves dividing the day into blocks of time, each allocated to a specific task or group of tasks. This helps to combat the tendency to multitask and become distracted. By dedicating specific time slots to certain activities and sticking to these allocations, you can create a more predictable and structured workday. Concentrating on one task at a time, you can make sure that each task receives the attention and effort it deserves.

One proponent of time blocking is Cal Newport, author of "Deep Work", who advocates for this technique as a means to enable more focused and productive work. By scheduling time for uninterrupted work, individuals can engage in deeper, more concentrated work sessions.

In addition to allocating specific times for individual tasks, Time Blocking can be further optimised by grouping similar tasks together in a single block. This approach, often referred to as 'Task Batching,' enhances efficiency by reducing the mental load and time lost in shifting gears between different types of work. For example, you might group all your email correspondence into one time block, dedicate another block for creative tasks like writing or design, and set aside a different period for meetings.

Task Batching works effectively because it capitalises on the brain's ability to maintain a flow state within a particular type of task. By focusing on similar tasks in one time block, you minimise the cognitive dissonance that often accompanies task-switching. This not only speeds up the completion of these tasks but also reduces mental fatigue, allowing for more sustained focus and productivity throughout the day.

Moreover, Time Blocking can be adapted to align with your natural energy levels throughout the day. By scheduling demanding tasks during your peak energy times and less intensive tasks during your lower energy periods, you can work with your body's natural rhythm, enhancing overall efficiency and effectiveness.

Implementing Time Blocking requires anticipating the tasks you need to accomplish, and understanding how much time each task or group of tasks will likely take. It also requires discipline to stick to the designated time blocks and resist the temptation to overrun them or get sidetracked by unscheduled tasks.

MANAGER VS MAKER

The concept of 'maker days' and 'manager days' has become increasingly popular in productivity circles, especially among professionals who balance diverse roles that require different types of focus and skills. This approach was popularised by computer scientist and entrepreneur Paul Graham in his essay "Maker's Schedule, Manager's Schedule."

In a 'maker day', the focus is on creative and intensive tasks that require uninterrupted blocks of time. Makers — like writers, developers, designers, or artists — often need half a day or more to immerse themselves in their work, finding their flow, and producing something of value. The maker's schedule can be disrupted by meetings and interruptions, which fragment time and impede deep work. This might mean limiting meetings, turning off notifications, or setting an autoresponder to manage expectations around availability.

Conversely, 'manager days' are structured around a different rhythm — one that is more fragmented, consisting of meetings, emails, and other administrative tasks. The stereotypical manager often switches between tasks and needs to be available for impromptu problem-solving and decision-making. On a manager day, the schedule is likely to be divided into one-hour blocks, each allocated to different meetings, calls, or administrative tasks. The success of a manager day lies in effective scheduling, ensuring that each block of time is used efficiently and aligns with broader goals and deadlines.

POPULAR TIME MANAGEMENT AND PLANNING TECHNIQUES

Choose your 'manager days' and your 'maker days'.

As a remote worker, you might designate certain days of the week as maker days, where you focus on deep, uninterrupted work. These days would have minimal meetings and would be dedicated to progressing on key projects or creative tasks. Other days could be manager days, focusing on collaboration, meetings, and administrative tasks that require immediate attention but less focused creativity. If you have a hybrid arrangement, you can extend your manager day to those days when you need to be in the office and focus on building relationships in other parts of the organisation. Conversely, if your reason for working from home is to avoid the commute, but find it difficult to concentrate there for long stretches of time, turn your office days into maker days.

THE REMOTE WORK ADD-ON: SYNCHRONOUS VS ASYNCHRONOUS TASKS

Tammy Bjelland, a notable voice in the field of remote work and founder of Workplaceless, categorises work into four distinct types based on two key factors: whether the work is asynchronous or synchronous, and whether it tolerates distractions. By categorising tasks into one of these groups, you can plan your work schedule and environment to align with the nature of the tasks you're undertaking.

Synchronous work refers to activities where participants interact in real-time, such as meetings or phone calls, requiring immediate engagement and response.

Asynchronous work, on the other hand, involves tasks or communications that do not require real-time interaction, allowing participants to engage with the work and respond to communication at their own convenience. (We will come back to the importance of asynchronous communication in remote work in Chapter 9.)

Tammy categorises the tasks as follows:

- **Asynchronous work that tolerates distractions**. These are tasks that don't require continuous, focused attention and can be done even with intermittent distractions. For example, administrative or repetitive tasks.
- **Synchronous or collaborative work that tolerates distractions.** This includes tasks that require real-time collaboration or discussions, where the presence of occasional distractions does not significantly impede the progress or outcome. It's about working alongside others in scenarios where the occasional interruption, such as a phone call or a quick question, can be accommodated without derailing the task at hand.
- **Asynchronous work that does not tolerate distractions.** This category includes tasks that require deep focus and concentration, best done in a distraction-free environment to

ensure quality and efficiency, like strategic thinking and work, or writing.
- **Synchronous work that does not tolerate distractions.** These are high-stakes, real-time interactions where full attention and professionalism are crucial, and distractions could significantly impact the effectiveness or outcome of the conversation or collaborative task.

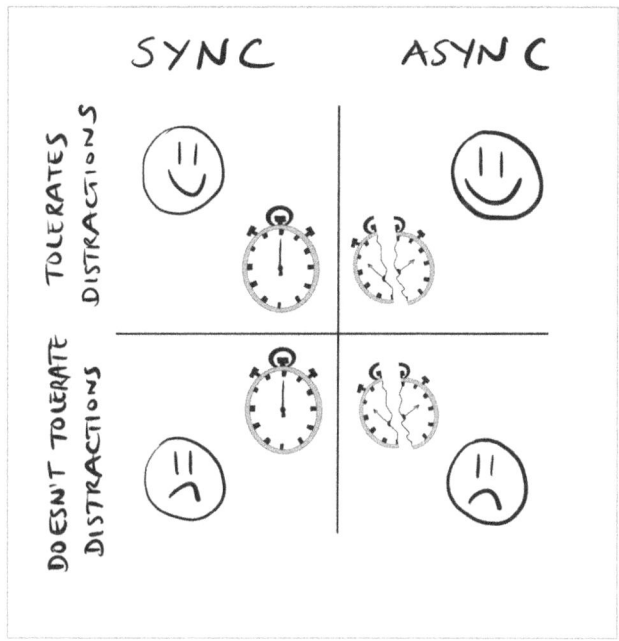

Consider whether your work can tolerate distractions.

Deciding which activities you need to do in real-time with others, and the level of distraction you can tolerate can help you plan your day.

QUICK CONTENT SUMMARY AND PRODUCTIVITY PATHFINDERS

This chapter is a bit different from previous ones, so let's give it a different ending.

Choose one technique to experiment with.

1. Prioritise with the Eisenhower Matrix: Review your task list and categorise each item using the Eisenhower Matrix. Decide what's urgent and important, and plan to tackle those tasks first.
2. Implement the Pomodoro Technique: Choose a task and work on it exclusively for 25 minutes. Afterward, take a five-minute break, then repeat the cycle.
3. Trial the 90-Minute Work Cycle: Identify a task that requires deep focus and dedicate a 90-minute block to it without interruptions. Follow it with a restful break to recharge.
4. Experiment with Time Blocking: Schedule your day into distinct blocks dedicated to specific tasks or types of work, and stick to these times as closely as possible.
5. Practice Task Batching: Group similar tasks together and complete them within a designated time block to minimise the mental load of switching between different types of tasks.
6. Designate Maker vs Manager Days: If possible, set entire days or half days focused on deep work (Maker days) and days filled with meetings and administrative tasks (Manager days).
7. Assess Task Nature: Determine whether your tasks for the week are synchronous or asynchronous and plan your work schedule around these distinctions.

CHAPTER 7
LESS POPULAR TIME MANAGEMENT STRATEGIES

It's now time to explore the less trodden but equally important paths of productivity strategies that hinge on the challenging aspect of boundary setting.

The focus of this chapter is on how to define and maintain both physical and temporal boundaries within different work environments. Setting boundaries extends beyond physical space—it encompasses the management of time and expectations with colleagues and clients in the digital space.

DEFINING YOUR BOUNDARIES

"Boundaries are to protect life, not to limit pleasures." – Edwin Louis Cole

While the concept of setting boundaries is popular and often discussed when talking about productivity in remote work, its actual implementation is a challenge. While the idea is widely endorsed for its benefits in work-life balance and mental well-being, putting it into practice effectively demands a careful blend of assertiveness, clarity, and consistency.

For example, in a home setting, setting up physical boundaries can be as simple as dedicating a specific room or a designated area as your workspace. This space should be exclusively for work, to create a mental association that when you are in this space, it's time for professional activities. In smaller living spaces, even a dedicated corner or a portable divider can serve this purpose. The physical separation helps in minimising interruptions from household activities and also aids in mentally switching off from work during off-hours.

Temporal boundaries are equally important. Setting fixed work hours mimics the structure of a traditional office and helps in maintaining a regular routine. Additionally, adhering to these hours prevents overworking, a common pitfall for those who find it hard to disconnect from work.

In coworking spaces, while the physical boundaries are inherently established by the nature of the space, maintaining temporal boundaries can be more challenging due to the presence of others working at different paces. It's beneficial to set personal work hours and take regular breaks as you would at home. The social aspect of coworking spaces, though beneficial for networking, should be balanced with the need for focused work time. Using headphones can signal to others that you are not available for casual interaction and also help you stay focused.

Cafés and public spaces offer a change of scenery and can boost creativity, but they also come with their own set of challenges in creating boundaries. Choosing a quiet time or a less crowded café can help.

For those who travel, maintaining these boundaries can be even more challenging due to changing environments. Using consistent tools like noise-canceling headphones or a portable laptop stand can create a sense of familiarity and boundary, irrespective of the location. Also, adhering to your regular work routine as much as possible while traveling helps in maintaining those temporal boundaries.

Establishing online boundaries

The boundaries we create for ourselves using our physical space are often crossed by people in other locations, who can't see what we're up to. That's what makes boundary setting as remote workers tricky. Letting those you interact with online know that you are not permanently available will stop them from expecting you to answer their messages immediately. The more you can communicate when you are available to collaborators and clients, the better.

Including availability information in email signatures and shared calendars are popular strategies for communicating your work hours and availability. For example, you could add a note about your working hours in your email signature, as a subtle yet effective way to inform others of your availability. Your email signature could include a line such as, "My working hours are 8 AM to 4 PM London time. Emails received outside of these hours will be responded to during the next business day." This sets clear expectations for email response times without the need for constant reminders.

By keeping your shared calendar up-to-date with your work schedule, meetings, and out-of-office times, you provide colleagues with real-time insight into your availability and reduce the likelihood of being disturbed during your off-hours or deep work periods. (In some cases, you might want to have different strategies on how to communicate this with your team versus the rest of the organisation and external parties.)

In companies where shared calendars are the norm, you can block out time for focused work, breaks, or personal commitments, making these as visible as any other meeting. This practice not only helps in managing your own time effectively, but also signals to others when you are not available for impromptu calls or meetings.

WHEN TO SAY "NO" AND HOW

If you say "yes" to every project, opportunity and collaboration that comes your way, your work will be never ending, no matter how many tasks you plot in your Eisenhower Matrix. If you don't become skilled at saying "no" to others' requests when your plate is full, then your plate will always be piled up. And if your creative thoughts keep spiralling away and you act on every impulse to start a new venture… you'll be working out in Pomodoros well into the night.

Learning to decline requests or opportunities that don't align with your goals or capacity is not just about preserving time; it's about respecting your priorities and limits.

Many thought-leaders and productivity experts emphasise the importance of being selective with commitments. Greg McKeown, in his book "Essentialism: The Disciplined Pursuit of Less", advocates for the disciplined pursuit of less but better. He argues that by saying "no" to things that don't align with your highest contribution, you make room for activities that truly matter. This approach is about making trade-offs consciously and realising that saying "yes" to any opportunity by default is an indirect "no" to another potentially more impactful opportunity.

Brené Brown talks about the importance of boundaries. In her book "Daring Greatly", she states, "Daring to set boundaries is about having the courage to love ourselves, even when we risk disappointing others." This is particularly relevant in remote work settings where coworkers or clients can't see you're busy and might inadvertently place unreasonable demands on your time.

TEMPLATES FOR SAYING "NO" TO OTHERS

Learning how to turn down extra work from colleagues or declining meetings where you won't add value is a skill worth learning. The key to saying "no" is to do it tactfully and respectfully. It's not just about declining; it's about communicating your reasons in a way that is understood and respected. This might mean explaining your current workload, your focus on other priorities, or simply that you need to avoid overcommitment to maintain the quality of your work. If appropriate, follow up after some time to see if there's a way you can contribute or be involved in a less time-intensive manner.

Here are some tactics and some examples for declining extra work, and turning down meeting invitations.

Turning Down Extra Work from Colleagues

1. Emphasise current commitments.

"I appreciate you thinking of me for this project, but I'm currently at full capacity with [list your current projects or responsibilities]. I want to ensure I deliver the best quality work on these existing commitments."

2. Offer alternative solutions.

"While I can't take on the full project due to my current workload, I can [offer a smaller contribution, suggest another colleague, or provide resources]. Would that be helpful?"

3. Express interest for the future.

"This sounds like an interesting project, and I'd love to be considered for similar opportunities in the future. Right now, though, I need to focus on [current project/goal]."

Declining Meetings Where You Won't Add Value - or that won't add value to you

1. Clarify your role.

"Could you help me understand what my role would be in this meeting? I want to ensure I'm contributing effectively and not attending meetings where my presence isn't necessary."

2. Suggest an alternative format.

"I'm not sure if my input is needed for this meeting. Would it be possible for me to provide my thoughts or feedback via email or a brief report instead?"

3. Offer to attend if necessary.

"Based on the agenda, it seems my contribution may not be essential. I'm happy to attend if you think it's necessary, but otherwise, I will use that time to focus on [other tasks]. Please feel free to update me afterward if anything relevant comes up."

Remember, the goal is to communicate your decision in a way that maintains positive relationships and shows respect for both your time and the time of others.

SAYING "NO" TO YOURSELF

"Respect your own boundaries, even if others won't." – Anonymous

Sometimes the person you need to say "no" to is yourself. This might mean resisting the urge to take on additional projects that you are passionate about but don't have the capacity for. It can also mean acknowledging when you are overworking and need to step back.

For creative minds and self-starters, the challenge of setting boundaries often lies within. The drive to innovate and the constant influx of ideas can be as exhilarating as it is overwhelming. If you find yourself brimming with creative energy and entrepreneurial spirit, you'll need to learn to say "no" to your own impulses. This self-restraint involves recognising the fine line between productive creativity and overcommitment. It means being discerning about which ideas to pursue and having the wisdom to acknowledge your limits.

Balancing this enthusiasm with practicality is often difficult - it requires channeling your creative energy into selected projects that you can manage effectively, without compromising your well-being or the quality of your work.

NURTURING YOUR PROFESSIONAL RELATIONSHIPS

Saying "no" is easier if you already have a good relationship with your colleagues, and they know you're not just being unhelpful. When you work remotely, you need to be more deliberate about nurturing your relationships.

When colleagues trust each other, they are more likely to be receptive to each other's limitations and understandings. If you have invested time in building rapport with your colleagues, they are more likely to respect your decision when you explain that taking on more work could compromise the quality of your output or lead to burnout. They understand your commitment to quality and your usual work ethic, which makes it easier for them to accept your boundaries.

Here are some ways to nurture your relationships at work:

1. **Celebrate milestones and achievements:** Celebrating birthdays, work anniversaries, or team achievements can help strengthen bonds. You can organise a quick gathering online, or simply send a digital card for someone's birthday.
2. **Share regular updates and communication**: Keep your team updated on your progress with projects. Regular updates prevent misunderstandings and create a sense of reliability. (Hopefully your team already has a process to do this, but if not, let people know what you're up.)
3. **Offer help and support**: If you notice a team member struggling or know they are working on something within your expertise, offer your help. It's a great way to show support and solidify relationships. (Don't assume that just because people aren't asking for help, they wouldn't welcome it.)
4. **Create instructional or informational content**: If you have expertise in a certain area, creating and sharing instructional

videos, guides, or blog posts can be a great way to share knowledge and engage with colleagues indirectly.
5. **Collaborate on documents and projects:** Contributing to shared documents or projects can be a non-intrusive way to collaborate and build rapport. Look out for those times when team members or others ask for feedback or other contributions.
6. **Share resources and articles**: If you come across an article, video, or resource you think a colleague would find valuable or interesting, share it with them with a brief note on why you thought of them. This is a great way to show that you're thinking about their interests or professional growth.
7. **Attend trainings and workshops**: Participate in online training and workshops offered by your organisation. These are not only learning opportunities but also a platform to interact with colleagues from different teams.
8. **Have regular check-ins with team members**: Schedule regular one-on-one virtual meetings, or in person coffees with your team members. These don't always have to be work-related; they can simply be a time to catch up and see how the other person is doing. This helps in building a personal connection beyond just professional interaction.
9. **Join or create interest groups**: If your organisation has interest groups or communities of practice, consider joining one of them. If none of them are of interest, why not start one yourself? It's a great way to connect with people outside your team or direct circle.
10. **Leverage professional networking platforms:** Platforms like LinkedIn can be great for staying connected with broader professional circles. Share updates, write articles, or engage with content posted by others.

Having covered the very personal topics of boundaries and human connection, get ready now to address the role of technology in personal productivity.

In Part 3, we'll explore how to leverage apps to streamline your workflow and manage your tasks more efficiently. We'll also discuss strategies for taming the often overwhelming world of online collaboration platforms and communication tools, ensuring that technology serves as an ally in your pursuit of productivity and not a source of constant distraction.

QUICK CONTENT SUMMARY

- Creating physical and temporal boundaries in remote work.
- Techniques for saying "no" to manage workload effectively.
- Building and nurturing professional relationships remotely.

PRODUCTIVITY PATHFINDERS

1. Designate Your Workspace: If you haven't already, select a specific area in your home for work to establish a clear physical boundary that enhances focus and productivity.
2. Update Your Online Availability: Reflect your work hours in your email signature and on shared calendars to ensure others are aware of your availability.
3. Develop Templates for Declining Requests: Create and use templates for politely turning down requests or meetings, saving you time and maintaining professionalism.
4. Prepare for Part 3: Anticipate learning about the technological tools that can enhance your productivity in the next chapters, and consider how these might fit into the boundaries you have set for yourself.

PART 3: TECHNOLOGY

CHAPTER 8
NAVIGATING DIGITAL TOOLS FOR INDIVIDUAL PRODUCTIVITY

This chapter covers the defining features of digital tools that enhance our workday: their user-friendliness, integration capabilities with other applications, and their scalability to match our evolving career needs. We explore a mindful approach to selecting these tools, assessing their fit with our unique work journey.

More than a mere examination of tools, this chapter focuses on constructing a digital ecosystem that amplifies our productivity. It's about creating a digital workspace that not only elevates our efficiency but also enriches our work experience with less stress and more satisfaction.

THE QUEST FOR THE PERFECT PRODUCTIVITY TOOL

Searching for the right tools can feel like a magical quest, so let's embark on this chapter with the epic journey of a fellow worker in her pursuit of the perfect tool.

Once upon a time, in the mystical land of Remoteworkia, there lived a diligent professional named Elena. In this realm, where mythical creatures roamed and magic was the norm, Elena's tasks ranged from the valiant - like dragon-slaying, known in our world as "meeting tight deadlines," to the arcane, such as potion-making or as we might say, "crafting meticulous reports." But even for someone as skilled as Elena, the challenge of managing her time and tasks efficiently was daunting.

Elena's quest for the ultimate productivity tool began on a bright, crisp morning. She ventured into the bustling Marketplace of Apps, a labyrinthine bazaar alive with merchants peddling software, each promising to vanquish the demons of inefficiency and disorder.

Armed with wisdom from the ancient and revered Productivity Oracle, Elena knew to seek not the shiniest tool, but the one that resonated with her soul. "Choose not for glitter or glamour," the Oracle had intoned, "but for that which echoes the rhythm of your heart and the cadence of your tasks."

Her journey first led her to the renowned stall of 'ListMaster 3000', where enchanted tools gleamed under the morning sun. This tool, famed for its intricate features and labyrinthine algorithms, was the choice of many a noble warrior in Remoteworkia. But as Elena peered into its depths, she found its complexity not a beacon, but a bewildering maze. It was a tool for commanders of vast armies, not for a solitary warrior like her.

Disheartened but not defeated, Elena wandered deeper into the marketplace and stumbled upon the humble abode of 'SimpleTasks'. This tool, cloaked in simplicity and praised for its minimalistic design, seemed the antithesis of ListMaster 3000. Yet, as Elena delved into its features, she found it lacked the alchemy to merge with the mystical scrolls of Google and the enchanted books of Outlook. SimpleTasks was a mere scribe's tool, not fit for the multifaceted quests Elena undertook.

As the sun began to dip below the horizon, casting long shadows over Remoteworkia, Elena's steps grew weary. She wondered if her quest was in vain. But in the fading light, she glimpsed a modest stall, veiled in a shimmering aura. Here lay 'Forever-Done', unassuming in appearance yet radiating a quiet power.

With a cautious hand, Elena reached for Forever-Done. In an instant, she felt a connection - an intuitive understanding flowed between her and the tool. Its interface was simple yet powerful, a perfect blend of functionality and ease. It promised seamless integration with her existing magical tools, merging her tasks, meetings, and deadlines into one harmonious tapestry.

Forever-Done was adaptable, evolving with Elena's needs. As her quests grew from mere potion-making to grand adventures of project management, Forever-Done was her steadfast companion, a beacon in the chaotic seas of Remoteworkia.

Just as Elena discovered with 'Forever-Done', the process of choosing the right personal productivity tool is not about being swayed by the dazzling array of options or the allure of popular choices. It's a thoughtful expedition, much like Elena's, into understanding one's own work habits, preferences, and the unique demands of one's tasks.

The key lies in finding a tool that complements and enhances your natural workflow, just as 'Forever-Done' did for Elena, transforming her work life into a harmonious blend of efficiency and satisfaction. This search involves several considerations, from the tool's ease of use and integration capabilities to its customisation options and scalability, all aimed at enhancing productivity.

When selecting personal productivity tools, it helps to adopt a thoughtful and personalised mindset.

1. Begin by reflecting on your work style

Do you thrive with a simple, straightforward interface, or do you require a tool that offers a range of features and customisation options? The tool you choose should naturally complement your workflow, fitting into it like a missing puzzle piece, rather than reshaping the way you work.

A tool that is intuitive and user-friendly can be a joy to use, while one that requires a steep learning curve or that leaves you frustrated might not be worth the investment of your time and energy. The ideal tool should feel like an extension of your thought process, enabling you to work efficiently rather than becoming a barrier.

If you have a specific way of working, you'll need a tool that you can customise heavily. The ability to tailor a tool to your specific needs, whether through customisable views, task categorisation options, or other personalised settings, can enhance your productivity. Customisation allows the tool to fit more snugly into your unique work pattern, making your work process more efficient and intuitive.

2. Consider which tools you're already using

The ability of a tool to seamlessly integrate with other applications and platforms you regularly use, such as email clients, calendars, or file storage services, can streamline your workflow. This integration ensures that your work ecosystem functions as a cohesive unit, rather than a disjointed collection of independent applications.

3. Think long-term

If you want to avoid switching tools constantly year on year, choose a tool that can adapt and grow with your evolving tasks and responsibilities, especially if your role or workload is dynamic. A tool that serves you well today should also be able to meet your needs tomorrow as your career grows and evolves.

You might also want to be cautious about adopting newly released software. Behind the initial launch, there can be a rush to release the first version, which might lead to issues or incomplete features. Furthermore, there's always the uncertainty of whether the tool might be acquired by a larger corporation and potentially shelved or drastically changed. To approach this 'longevity measure,' look for tools with a proven track record of consistent updates and positive user feedback. It's also beneficial to research the company's history and its product development roadmap to gauge future reliability and support.

4. Beware new, shiny things

Finally, avoid being swayed by popularity alone. Just because a tool is widely used or has rave reviews doesn't necessarily mean it's the right fit for your specific needs. Focus on how well it aligns with your unique requirements, work style, and the nature of your tasks.

"Technology is a useful servant but a dangerous master."
– Christian Lous Lange

ESSENTIAL TYPES OF DIGITAL TOOLS

A contemporary book on Time Management wouldn't be complete without covering productivity digital tools.

While this guide won't specifically name tools — largely because the digital landscape is constantly evolving, with new tools emerging and others becoming obsolete — it's worth spending a few lines on looking at how to best use some foundational apps. So let's have a look at three types of tools widely use amongst knowledge workers (note-taking apps, to-do lists and calendars), and how to make the best out of them.

Note-taking apps

- **Organise notes by categories or projects.** Use folders or tagging features to categorise your notes. This organisation makes it easier to retrieve information when needed.
- **Sync across devices**. Ensure your note-taking app syncs across all devices, to allow you to capture thoughts or ideas regardless of whether you're at your desk or on the move.
- **Regularly review and cleanup.** Set aside time weekly or monthly to review and clean up your notes. This habit prevents accumulation of irrelevant information and keeps your digital space clear and manageable.

To-Do List mastery

- **Prioritise tasks.** Use features like colour coding or prioritisation flags to highlight urgent or important tasks. This visual organisation helps with focusing on high-priority items first.
- **Break down large tasks.** For complex tasks, break them down into smaller, actionable steps. This breakdown makes the tasks less daunting and more manageable.
- **Update regularly.** Keep your to-do list dynamic. Add new tasks as they come and remove completed ones. Regular updates ensure that the list always reflects current priorities.

Calendar management

- **Set reminders for important deadlines.** Use the reminder or alert functions to notify you of upcoming deadlines or meetings. These reminders can help in better time management and prevent last-minute rushes.
- **Schedule downtime.** Remember to block time for breaks, lunch, and even end-of-day wind-down time. Scheduling these periods ensures you don't overlook self-care and rest.

There are two more types of tools that can help you organise your time: project management tools and time tracking software. These are usually used at a team or organisational level, but they can also be used by you as an individual. When harnessed properly, these tools are not just about keeping tabs on what's done and what's pending; they're also about gaining profound insights into your own work patterns.

PROJECT MANAGEMENT TOOLS

Two types of tools to help you visualise your work are Gantt charts and Kanban boards.

A Gantt chart is a type of bar chart that illustrates a project schedule, showing the start and finish dates of various elements of a project. It's

NAVIGATING DIGITAL TOOLS FOR INDIVIDUAL PRODUCTIVI... 83

like a timeline that maps out your project journey, allowing you to see how different tasks overlap and relate to each other over time.

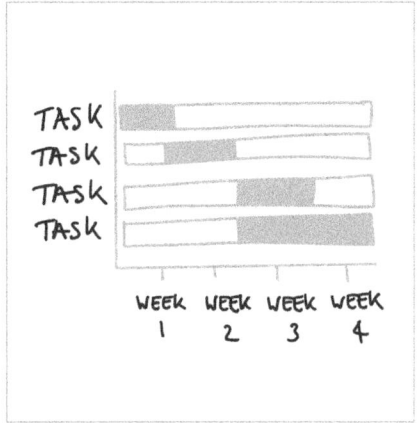

A simple Gantt chart.

On the other hand, a Kanban board is a visual tool that helps to manage workflow. It typically consists of columns labeled with stages of the process, such as 'To Do', 'In Progress', and 'Done'. Tasks are represented as cards that move from one column to the next, visually tracking the progress of work through each stage.

A Kanban board.

Both Gantt charts and Kanban boards are not only tools for organisation; they provide a clear and immediate overview of where things stand, making them invaluable for effective project management. If visual tracking of your tasks helps you organise your time and drives your motivation, take the time to explore the latest apps and platforms offering these functionalities. Delving into the current tech landscape can uncover tools that perfectly align with your work style and goals.

∼

TIME TRACKING: BEYOND THE CLOCK

Often perceived as a mere clock-watching exercise, time tracking can be a window into your work habits. Integrating time tracking into your routine is less about counting hours and more about understanding them.

When you start tracking your time, patterns emerge. You begin to notice during which part of the day you're most productive, which tasks consume most of your energy, and importantly, when you need to step back and recharge. This self-awareness is key in remote work where the lines between professional and personal life often blur.

But there's also a subtler aspect of time tracking – it's about self-honesty. Are you spending too much time on tasks that don't align with your primary goals? Are meetings eating into your creative time? This level of introspection can lead to powerful shifts in how you manage your day.

To start tracking your time effectively, follow these steps:

1. **Choose a time tracking tool**

Select a time tracking app or software that suits your needs. There are various options available, ranging from simple stopwatch apps to more comprehensive tools that can categorize tasks and generate reports. Look for a tool that is user-friendly and integrates well with other tools you use. A simple chart on a piece of paper will also do!

2. **Define your tasks**

Break down your workday into specific tasks or categories. These could include project work, meetings, emails, breaks, and even non-work activities. Being specific helps in accurately assessing how you spend your time.

3. **Set a routine**

Decide when you will track your time. Will you start and stop the tracker as you switch tasks, or will you log hours at the end of the day? Consistency is key, so choose a method that feels sustainable for you.

4. **Record diligently**

For the first few weeks, track everything. Yes, everything. The more data you have, the clearer the picture of your work habits will be. Include even small tasks or breaks to get a comprehensive overview.

5. **Review regularly**

Set aside time each week to review your time tracking data. Look for patterns: when are you most productive, which tasks take longer than expected, and when do you tend to lose focus? You can use this information to adjust your schedule and work habits.

6. **Make adjustments**

Use the insights gained from your time tracking to make informed decisions about your work. You might need to reallocate your time, change your work routine, or eliminate unnecessary tasks.

7. **Seek balance**

Remember, time tracking is not just about work efficiency. It's also about finding a balance. Make sure you're allocating time for breaks, personal development, and relaxation.

By following these steps, you can turn time tracking from a mere exercise in clock-watching to a powerful tool for personal and professional growth. Remember, the goal is not to micromanage every minute but to gain a better understanding of your work habits and improve your overall productivity and work-life relationship.

The next chapter will focus on mastering online collaboration platforms and communication tools, and how to harness these digital tools in ways that tame their potentially overwhelming nature.

QUICK CONTENT SUMMARY

- Selecting the right personal productivity tools.
- Effective use of note-taking apps and to-do lists.
- Efficient calendar management for time blocking and scheduling.

PRODUCTIVITY PATHFINDERS

1. Assess Your Digital Toolkit: Take an inventory of all the digital tools you currently use. Determine which ones serve your needs well and which ones could be replaced or eliminated.
2. Experiment with New Tools: Based on your assessment, identify potential new tools that might enhance your

productivity. Experiment with them one at a time to avoid overwhelming your routine.
3. Monitor Your Usage: Pay attention to how you use your digital tools over a week. Look for patterns or habits that either contribute to or detract from your productivity.
4. Simplify When Possible: If you find that a tool is too complex or isn't being used to its full potential, consider simplifying your toolkit. Sometimes less is more when it comes to productivity tools.

CHAPTER 9
CONTROL THE TECH BEFORE IT CONTROLS YOU

As we approach the end of the book, it's time to confront one of the most widespread challenge for remote workers: mastering technology to ensure it serves us as a tool, rather than becoming an overbearing presence in our work lives. When collaborating with others, technology can significantly enhance our work efficiency - but it also has the potential to overwhelm us and encroach upon our personal lives.

This chapter equips you with the tools and strategies to navigate the digital landscape of remote work confidently. By controlling the technology you use before it controls you, you can maintain your focus, enhance your productivity, and, importantly, preserve your mental space for the things that truly matter.

A QUARTET OF COMMUNICATION ESSENTIALS

Regardless of the nature of your job, as a remote worker you're likely to encounter three different types of communication tools. This section addresses how to manage them effectively.

Email: the tool that won't go away

Email is a double-edged sword. It's essential for communication but can quickly become a source of constant distraction. Moreover, the habit of constantly checking emails can be counterproductive. Research suggests that limiting email checks to specific times during the day can reduce distractions and increase productivity. This doesn't mean ignoring your inbox; rather, it's about setting specific intervals for email management, allowing for prolonged periods of focused work.

Instant messaging: balancing responsiveness with focus

Instant messaging platforms, while invaluable for quick communication, can also be a major source of interruption. The key to leveraging these tools effectively is finding the balance between being responsive and maintaining focus. One approach is to designate 'quiet hours' during which your notifications are muted. If you're working in a team, agreeing on a common 'responsiveness schedule' can help you all find time for focused work.

"Instant messaging is the 21st-century version of passing notes in school." – Anonymous

Online meetings: you can't live with (too many of) them, you can't live without them

Video calls have become a staple in remote work, but they can also consume a disproportionate amount of time if not managed well. Effective meetings have a clear agenda and adhere to predetermined time limits - unless you agree otherwise. Needless to say, make sure you are on time and ensure your video and audio is as good as it can be.

Remember, and remind others, that not every discussion requires a video call. Sometimes, an email, a quick phone call or an asynchronous message can suffice.

Try an 'async first' approach

Adopting an 'async first' approach to communication in remote work is about shifting your mindset from the need for immediate responses and constant connectivity to a more deliberate and thoughtful method of interaction. This approach doesn't necessarily mean abandoning real-time tools like instant messaging or frequent meetings; rather, it's about reevaluating the urgency and necessity of these interactions.

By prioritising asynchronous communication, such as emails or shared documents, for non-urgent matters, you allow yourself and your team members to respond thoughtfully in your own time, rather than being pulled away from focused work for immediate but non-critical issues. This shift encourages a culture where being 'always on' isn't the default expectation, fostering a more balanced and less interruptive work environment. Clearly communicating this approach with your team and external parties helps set healthy boundaries and expectations, contributing to a more efficient and focused workflow.

AVOIDING EXTERNAL INTERRUPTIONS

While digital communication tools are essential, they can become sources of distraction if not managed properly. Here are three simple tactics to reduce non-urgent interruptions throughout the day.

1. Customise notification settings

If you haven't yet tweaked the default settings in your apps, finish this paragraph, put the book down and take action. Select which notifications are important enough to warrant immediate attention. For instance, you might decide that only direct messages or emails from key team members or clients trigger an immediate alert, while others can be relegated to a less intrusive notification style or turned off entirely. Decide whether the default notification settings (usually pop-ups and pings) are useful, or annoying. If the latter, turn them off.

Get in the habit of customising notifications whenever you join a new platform or adopt a new collaboration tool.

2. Use 'do not disturb' modes

Most devices and messaging platforms offer a 'Do Not Disturb' (DND) feature. Activating DND mode silences non-critical notifications, allowing for uninterrupted concentration. It's a simple yet powerful tool that can be scheduled during your typical deep work hours or activated manually for impromptu focus sessions.

3. Batch processing of communications

Designate specific times for checking and responding to messages and emails. This method, often referred to as 'batch processing', consolidates communication tasks into defined blocks of time, rather than allowing them to scatter throughout the day. By scheduling these blocks at times when your energy or focus might naturally be lower, you can use your peak periods more effectively for tasks that require deeper concentration. (This is a version of the Task Batching method we discussed in Chapter 6.)

Regularly check the platforms where there might be messages for you - don't always rely on your notifications to alert you when messages are waiting, as sometimes notifications settings change during app or platform updates.

While we're in listicle mode, let's have a look at other ways of maintaining our focus amidst the technology that is so key to our work.

1. Mindful engagement with devices

Developing a habit of mindful engagement means being intentional about when and why you pick up your phone or switch tabs to a messaging app. Before reaching for your phone, pause and ask yourself if it's necessary at that moment, or if it can wait.

A study published in the journal "Computers in Human Behavior" (2015) found that mindfulness training helped reduce the frequency of compulsive internet use. This suggests that being more mindful and intentional about device use can mitigate compulsive checking behaviours. You don't need to adopt 'mindfulness practices' - you can simply honour the original meaning of 'being mindful'.

2. Physical separation from devices

Research led by Dr. Adrian Ward at the University of Texas at Austin demonstrated that the mere presence of a smartphone can reduce cognitive capacity, even when the phone is turned off, while Jeanette Skowronek and colleagues in Germany's Universität Paderborn demonstrated their presence can reduce our attention.

Sometimes, the simplest solution to control distractions is to physically separate yourself from your devices. If you find your phone is a constant source of distraction, try keeping it in another room or out of sight during work hours. This physical separation can significantly reduce the temptation to check it impulsively.

3. Creating a notification-free workspace

Establish a designated area of your workspace as a notification-free zone. When working in this area, all devices are either set to DND mode or are kept away. This can be especially effective in a home office setting, where the blending of personal and professional spaces often leads to increased distractions. Alternatively, you can select your café or coworking space as your DND environment.

4. Replace your phone with other gadgets

Finally, if you find yourself checking messages every time you pick up your phone to look at the time, buy a watch. And if turning off the alarm on your phone every morning leads you to checking emails before you've got out of bed, buy an alarm clock. Honestly.

THE DANGERS OF DIGITAL PRESENTEEISM

Jordan, a dedicated software developer, had fully embraced life as a remote worker. His workstation was set up in a quiet corner of his flat, overlooking a serene cityscape. The flexibility and comfort of working from home were things Jordan cherished deeply. However, as weeks turned into months, Jordan began to notice a subtle shift in his work habits.

It started with just answering a few emails after dinner. Then, it progressed to coding late into the night, often accompanied by the soft glow of his laptop screen. Jordan prided himself on his strong work ethic, but the boundaries between his professional and personal life were becoming increasingly blurred. Without Jordan realising it, his home had become an extension of his office - and it seemed to be open all hours.

The expectation to be constantly available had crept in unnoticed. He found himself responding to work queries late at night, setting a precedent for round-the-clock availability. The distinction between 'urgent' and 'can wait until morning' had become fuzzy.

One evening, as Jordan typed away long after most of the city had gone to sleep, he paused. He realised that the project he was working on wasn't urgent, and yet, there he was, sacrificing his rest for it. It was a moment of clarity for Jordan – his desire to show his dedication had morphed into a habit that was now encroaching on his personal time and well-being.

The following day, Jordan made a conscious decision. He set specific working hours and communicated these to his team. He began to use the 'Do Not Disturb' features on his messaging apps and email, carving out time for breaks and personal activities. Mentally, he reminded himself that his team knew that he was dedicated to his work - he didn't need to constantly "show his digital face".

Digital presenteeism, a phenomenon particularly prevalent in remote work environments, represents a significant challenge in today's workforce. Unlike traditional presenteeism, where employees might physically come to work even when unwell, or where the backs of chairs have coats permanently hanging off them, digital presenteeism involves being constantly connected and engaged with work through digital means, often beyond regular working hours. In addition to this, digital presenteeism is particularly challenging to detect and manage, as it lacks the visible cues of its traditional counterpart.

Research and thought leaders in the field of workplace productivity have highlighted the implications of digital presenteeism. A study by Virginia Tech, for instance, revealed that the mere expectation of having to check work emails during non-work hours can significantly increase anxiety and strain on employees.

The convenience and omnipresence of digital tools in remote work can indeed make it easier for you to be present and actively participate in your work environment. Digital presenteeism can lead to exhaustion and burnout, or can simply remove the joy from your work. Remember, being constantly connected does not equate to being more productive; in fact, it can be counterproductive, diminishing your overall well-being and effectiveness. An overworked and fatigued self is far from beneficial, both for you and your team.

Given the importance of early burnout recognition, let's identify and address the warning signs.

IDENTIFYING THE SYMPTOMS OF BURNOUT

Burnout, a state of emotional, physical, and mental exhaustion caused by prolonged stress, is particularly insidious in remote work settings. It often creeps in unnoticed, especially among those who are deeply passionate about their work or have a strong desire to meet and exceed expectations. These individuals may be more prone to burnout as their dedication and commitment can lead to consistently pushing beyond healthy limits.

In a traditional office, physical cues like colleagues taking breaks or the office emptying out signal the end of the workday. Remote workers, however, often lack these environmental prompts. This absence can lead to fewer breaks and longer work hours as the lines between 'work time' and 'personal time' blur.

Be vigilant for symptoms of chronic fatigue and emotional exhaustion, two hallmark signs of burnout. Chronic fatigue in this context differs significantly from the normal tiredness experienced after a strenuous day. It is a persistent state of physical and mental depletion that rest does not easily remedy. Emotional exhaustion is equally telling; it manifests as a profound sense of being emotionally drained and overwhelmed.

Burnout can also lead to a noticeable decline in productivity. Tasks that once felt engaging may now feel insurmountable. There's also a sense of detachment or cynicism towards work, where one's job no longer provides a sense of satisfaction or achievement.

To guard yourself against burnout, you can start to implement some of the strategies we've already covered in this book like:

- Establishing a structured daily routine with clear boundaries between work and personal time.
- Making time for breaks, physical exercise, and leisure activities.
- Defining a workspace that mentally signals 'work mode' and stepping away from this space during off hours.

If symptoms of burnout begin to surface, it's important to acknowledge them and consider seeking support from a mental health professional. You can also look into designing more sustainable work practices through open communication with your manager or colleagues about workload and stress levels. Remember, prioritising your well-being is not just beneficial for you but also for the quality of work you produce and the overall health of your team or organisation.

 "It's not information overload. It's filter failure." – Clay Shirky

QUICK CONTENT SUMMARY

- Managing online communication to avoid overload.
- Balancing responsiveness with focus in instant messaging.
- Adopting an 'async first' approach for efficient communication.
- Reducing digital interruptions through notification management.
- Identifying the symptoms of burnout.

PRODUCTIVITY PATHFINDERS

1. Audit Your Digital Usage: Reflect on how you currently use your digital tools and identify areas where you can improve your efficiency and reduce distractions.
2. Schedule Checks for Email/Other Messages: Set specific times in your day for checking emails and/or messages, avoiding the temptation to respond to every notification immediately.
3. Adopt an 'async first' Communication Style: Prioritise asynchronous communication to allow for thoughtful responses and reduce the pressure of instant availability.

4. Customise Notification Settings: Tailor your notification settings across all devices to minimise interruptions, only allowing alerts for high-priority items.
5. Plan for Digital Well-being: As we move into Part 4, start thinking about the long-term changes you want to make in your relationship with technology, and how you can continue to improve your remote work practices to support your overall well-being.

We've now reached the end of Part 3, so get ready to start thinking about how to make the most out of this book by embedding some of its principles into your long-term practice. Part 4 is dedicated to applying the principles learned, making lasting changes, and fostering an environment for ongoing growth and development in our personal and professional lives.

PART 4: TRANSFORMATION

CHAPTER 10
PROGRESS AND TRANSFORMATION

We're nearly there.

This final chapter isn't merely a conclusion; it's an invitation to continue with your self-improvement and to reimagine the way we work.

Without the structured learning opportunities found in an office, you must be proactive in seeking growth and intentionally refine your work habits. To future-proof your remote work experience you'll need to embrace change while staying grounded, and discerning which trends and tools truly add value to your work and life.

Chapter 10 is not just about looking back on what you've learned; it's about looking forward to the transformation that awaits. It's about choosing from some of the concepts and tactics you've learned from this book and applying them to create a work experience that's continually evolving, deeply satisfying, and truly yours. As the last chapter in the book, this is your springboard to a future where you control your work, rather than letting it control you.

"Education is not the filling of a pail, but the lighting of a fire." – W.B. Yeats

Working away from others can prove challenging when it comes to personal and professional development. Unlike traditional office settings, where learning and development opportunities may be more structured or directly influenced by daily interactions with colleagues and supervisors, remote workers need to drive their own development.

This isn't just about honing the skills required for your specific job role; it's about refining how you work in a remote environment. While tools, techniques, and external guidance can provide a framework, the real growth happens when you actively engage in self-evaluation and take conscious steps to enhance your work habits and practices. Whether it's mastering time management, improving communication, or developing a healthier work-life dynamic, it's your responsibility to identify areas for growth and actively seek ways to improve.

THE ESSENCE OF ONGOING DEVELOPMENT

 "We do not learn from experience... we learn from reflecting on experience." – John Dewey

Ongoing development involves regularly examining your work processes, tools, and strategies to identify areas for enhancement. It's about asking yourself, "Is there a better way to do this?" or "What can I learn from recent experiences?". This mindset of seeking growth and learning from both success and failure is what drives meaningful progress.

In practice, this might mean seeking regular feedback from your team or clients, or blocking out time during the week to reading and thinking deeply about future trends. Here are some ways in which you can embed learning into your work time.

Embracing mistakes as learning opportunities.

Mistakes, often seen as setbacks, are actually powerful catalysts for growth. Reframing them as learning opportunities can help you prevent similar errors in the future - as well as softening the blow.

As a remote worker, where you often navigate tasks independently, mistakes can feel more pronounced. However, adopting a growth mindset can transform the way you perceive these errors. Instead of viewing mistakes as reflections of your abilities, see them as opportunities to expand your skill set and knowledge base. It's about asking, "What can I learn from this?" rather than "Why did I fail?".

The power of feedback in shaping your path.

Feedback, whether it comes from colleagues, managers, or clients, is an invaluable source of insight and growth, and requires a proactive and open approach. Unfortunately, when we work away from others, informal feedback is difficult to come by, so you will need to be proactive in seeking it.

You can seek feedback through formal mechanisms like performance reviews or informal channels like post-project discussions. If you work with clients, or you are involved with different teams in your organisation, you can also use a survey tool to set up a form you regularly send out.

When receiving feedback, especially if it's critical, focus on the actionable aspects. What specific changes can you make based on this feedback? How can it help you move closer to your goals?

Integrate learning into your workflow.

Establish a routine for self-review. This could be weekly, monthly, or quarterly. During these reviews, reflect on your recent work experiences. What tasks did you excel at? Where did you encounter challenges? What feedback have you received, and how can you incorporate it into your work?

You could also set aside time for reflection after completing a project, where you analyse both what went well and what could have been done better. Sharing these reflections and learnings with your team can also be helpful and strengthen your relationships.

Stay informed and adapt.

The remote work environment is continually changing, with new tools and methodologies emerging regularly. There's now also more and more research about remote work in the current landscape, supporting or dispelling "best practices". You can stay informed about these developments by subscribing to relevant newsletters, joining professional networks, and listening to podcasts. This habit will not only inspire new ideas but also keep you adaptable to changing trends, so make sure you block time in your calendar for staying informed.

Focus on your health and wellness.

Your physical and mental health play a crucial role in your productivity and job satisfaction. Incorporate regular physical activity into your routine, make sure you get enough good quality sleep, and ensure you're eating healthily. Regular health check-ins are as crucial as professional ones.

While you should definitely carry out activities you enjoy the most, consider those you've never tried before. While there is value in learning within your comfort zone, stepping into the unknown can also unlock new and unexpected avenues of learning. This balance between comfort and challenge is key to a well-rounded and enriching learning experience.

JOURNALING FOR GROWTH

Maintaining a personal learning journal can be an effective way to document and process the lessons from your experiences. Over time, this journal can become a valuable resource, offering insights into your growth trajectory and helping you track the evolution of your skills and approaches. For some people, keeping a record of their growth is a motivator to continue investing in their learning practice. If this sounds like you, consider maintaining a journal to document your learnings, ideas, and reflections.

To make journaling a part of your routine, set aside a regular time for it – perhaps at the end of the workday or week. Keep your journal (digital or physical) in a place that's easily accessible. Remember, the key to effective journaling is consistency and honesty.

Here are some of the things you can include:

Documenting learning experiences.

Each entry serves as a snapshot of a particular day or project. You record not only what happened but also how you approached problems, the solutions you devised, and the outcomes of those solutions. This practice helps in capturing real-time reflections and reactions, which are often lost in hindsight.

In her book "How to Have a Good Day", Caroline Webb discusses a piece of research conducted at a call centre in India. During a four-week training period, new recruits received identical training. However, a subset of these recruits were instructed to spend fifteen minutes each day writing down key lessons they learned. When tested after the training, these employees performed 23 percent better than their peers who did not engage in daily reflective writing.

Analysing mistakes and successes.

More than just a record of events, the journal allows for deep analysis. When a project doesn't go as planned, jotting down your thoughts on what went wrong and why can provide clarity. Conversely, when things go well, noting down the reasons for your success can be equally enlightening. This analysis helps in identifying patterns in your work behaviour, both positive and negative.

Emotional processing.

The act of writing can be therapeutic. It provides an outlet to express and process the emotions associated with your work – be it frustration from a setback or excitement from a breakthrough.

Setting and reviewing goals.

Your journal can also be a space for setting short-term and long-term goals. Regularly reviewing these goals and noting your progress towards them can be motivating. It also allows you to course-correct if you find yourself straying from your intended path.

Sharing and collaboration.

While primarily a personal tool, your learning journal can also be a resource for collaboration and sharing. Insights gleaned from your journal can be valuable in team retrospectives or mentoring sessions, helping others learn from your experiences.

Remember, your journal doesn't have to be limited to written entries. If you're someone who processes thoughts more effectively through sketching, doodling, or playing with colours on a page, embrace these visual methods in your journaling practice. For those who find clarity in speaking over writing, maintaining an audio diary can be an excellent alternative.

"Journal writing is a voyage to the interior." – Christina Baldwin

CONDUCTING A WEEKLY REVIEW

If journaling does not suit your personality or schedule, consider reviewing your practice weekly. Here are some guidelines to help you run a weekly review.

1. Set aside dedicated time

Choose a consistent day and time each week for your review. Popular times are Friday afternoons or Sunday evenings, but you get to choose when your week starts - just make sure it happens at the same time every week to make the review a habit. Ensure this is uninterrupted time where you can focus solely on the review process.

2. Review completed tasks and projects

Start by looking back at what you accomplished during the week. Go through your task lists, calendars, and project management tools. Acknowledge the progress made, even if it's smaller than expected. This step provides a sense of closure and accomplishment.

3. Evaluate goals and objectives

Reflect on your broader goals and objectives. How does your week's work align with these? This is a time to step back and look at the bigger picture, assessing whether your daily activities are moving you in the right direction.

4. Identify challenges and learning points

Consider any challenges you faced. Were there obstacles that hindered your progress? Reflect on what you learned from these challenges and how you can apply these lessons in the future. This could involve strategic adjustments or personal development goals.

5. **Plan for the upcoming week**

With the insights gained from your review, start planning for the next week. Prioritise tasks and set realistic goals. If certain tasks were not completed in the past week, decide if they should be carried over or reassessed.

6. **Self-care and well-being check**

End your review by assessing your physical and mental well-being. Are you taking enough breaks? Are you getting enough exercise and sleep? This reflection ensures that self-care remains a priority.

A weekly review is more than just a planning session; it's a holistic process that encompasses task management, goal alignment, learning, and personal well-being.

FUTURE-PROOFING YOUR REMOTE WORK EXPERIENCE

Staying updated with the latest technology trends and looking into the future of work is not just about maintaining relevance; it's about continually rediscovering the joy and potential of this dynamic mode of work. As remote workers, we have the unique opportunity to redefine the workspace, to blend the boundaries of professional and personal life in a way that fosters our growth, satisfaction, and well-being. However, this also requires a mindful approach to prevent being overwhelmed by the very technology and practices that are meant to empower us.

Each new trend, tool, or practice is a chance to enhance our work experience. Imagine the freedom of working from a cosy home office or a bustling cafe, the flexibility to structure your day to match your productivity rhythms, and the opportunity to connect with colleagues and clients across the globe. These are the hallmarks of remote work that continue to attract and inspire many.

Yet, with this freedom comes the responsibility of self-regulation. The digital nature of remote work can sometimes lead us down a path of constant connectivity, where the line between being productive and being perpetually plugged in becomes blurred. It's easy to get caught up in the latest productivity tools or practices, believing that more technology equates to better work. However, true productivity in remote work is about finding the right balance – leveraging technology to enhance our work without letting it dominate our lives.

Staying grounded while embracing change

Staying updated with remote working trends means more than just keeping pace with technological advancements; it's about discerning which trends align with your work style and values. It's about adopting tools and practices that resonate with you and enhance your work, not just because they are popular or new. Remember to periodically step back and assess their impact on your work and life.

Does a new tool bring efficiency and ease, or does it add unnecessary complexity? Are the latest time management practices helping you achieve a better work-life relationship, or are they adding more to your plate? These reflections can help you make conscious choices that align with your personal and professional goals.

FINAL WORDS

The beauty of remote work lies in its inherent flexibility and the empowerment it offers to tailor your work environment. This is a mode of work that celebrates individuality and autonomy, but that can also help you to connect with the best collaborators. It's an invitation to craft a work life that not only achieves professional goals but also supports personal well-being and happiness.

Take a moment to appreciate this unique work culture you are part of – one that breaks free from the confines of traditional office spaces and conventional work hours, offering a canvas to design a work life that brings happiness to all.

∼

QUICK CONTENT SUMMARY

- Emphasising ongoing self-evaluation and development.
- Learning from mistakes and integrating feedback.
- Embedding continuous learning into daily routines.
- Maintaining physical and mental health for sustained productivity.
- Strategies for journaling to capture growth and insights.

∼

A FINAL CALL TO ACTION

Your development as a remote worker is a testament to the efficacy of this mode of work.

Your growth can contribute to the collective proof that remote work is not just a viable alternative, but a superior way of life for many. Keep pushing the boundaries of what you can achieve from the place you feel most comfortable, most inspired.

By continually improving, you're not just advancing your own career —you're also reinforcing the message that remote work is the fertile ground for unmatched productivity and satisfaction. So, rise to the occasion, and let every step you take in bettering your work habits be a resounding affirmation that remote work truly works.

REFERENCES

Becker, William J. et al. "Killing me softly: Electronic communications monitoring and employee and spouse well-being." Academy of Management Proceedings (2018)

Brown, B. (2015). Daring Greatly: How the Courage to Be Vulnerable Transforms the Way We Live, Love, Parent, and Lead. Penguin Life.

Cameron, J. (2020). The Artist's Way: A Spiritual Path to Higher Creativity. Souvenir Press.

Covey, S. R. (1989). The 7 Habits of Highly Effective People. Simon & Schuster.

Flett, G.L., Stainton, M., Hewitt, P.L. et al. Procrastination Automatic Thoughts as a Personality Construct: An Analysis of the Procrastinatory Cognitions Inventory. Journal of Rational- Emotive & Cognitive Behaviour Therapy. 30, 223–236 (2012)

Graham, P. Maker's Schedule, Manager's Schedule. Available at https://www.paulgraham.com/makersschedule.html

Heaslip, E. (2020) quoting Bjeland, T. How to Manage Your Time When You're Working From Home. Available at https://www.uschamber.com/co/start/strategy/work-from-home-time-management-working-strategies

McIntyre, E., Wiener, K.K.K. and Saliba, A.J. (2015) 'Compulsive Internet use and relations between social connectedness, and introversion', Computers in Human Behavior, 48, pp. 569-574.

McKeown, G. (2021). Essentialism: The Disciplined Pursuit of Less. Virgin Books.

Ophir E, Nass C, Wagner AD. Cognitive control in media multitaskers. Proc Natl Acad Sci U S A. 2009 Sep 15;106(37):15583-7.

Schwartz, T., and Loehr, J. (2003). The Power of Full Engagement: Managing Energy, Not Time, Is the Key to High Performance and Personal Renewal. Simon and Schuster.

Skowronek, J., Seifert, A. and Lindberg, S. (2023) 'The mere presence of a smartphone reduces basal attentional performance', Scientific Reports, 13, 9363.

REFERENCES

Tice, D. M. and Baumeister, R. F. Longitudinal Study of Procrastination, Performance, Stress, and Health: The Costs and Benefits of Dawdling. Psychological Science. Vol. 8, No. 6 (Nov., 1997), pp. 454-458

Ward, A.F., Duke, K., Gneezy, A. and Bos, M.W. (2017) 'Brain drain: The mere presence of one's own smartphone reduces available cognitive capacity', Journal of the Association for Consumer Research, 2(2), pp. 140-154.

Williams Yost, C. (2004) Work + Life: Finding the Fit That's Right for You. Riverhead Books.

ACKNOWLEDGMENTS

Hi, Pilar here.

I'm finding writing this section more interesting than writing it for my other books, as this has been an unusually solitary endeavour - except for my partnership with ChatGPT.

I've written, edited and published the book *mainly* with the help of technology - no other humans were harmed in the process!

However, it would be remiss of me not to acknowledge all the people who have directly or indirectly helped and supported me through this.

The reason why I say that I wrote the book *mainly* with the help of technology is that my friend Mark Kilby, author of "From Chaos to Successful Distributed Agile Teams", provided me with an absolute gift just as I was about to publish the book. After reading the full manuscript, Mark gave me a list of 'gifts' and 'greats' and content suggestions I have integrated. If you are someone who struggles with giving feedback, I suggest you take a look at how he does it: https://www.markkilby.com/gifts-and-greats-for-true-feedback/ His 'book review' was certainly a gift - and working with a peer was more rewarding than working with tech.

I'd also like to thank Lisette Sutherland, author of "Work Together Anywhere", as she confirmed that I had something worth publishing and to Theresa Sigillito Hollema, author of "Virtual Teams Across Cultures" for her notes. And thanks to my mother, who focused on the language and confirmed that it was indeed, easy to read.

Many thanks to Hassan Osman, author of "Influencing Virtual Teams", for providing me with an endorsement for the book, and for role-modelling the writing of short, actionable books - those which he writes very well, but I could never write on my own.

There are others who've helped me indirectly: Joanna Penn, writer and host of "The Creative Penn" podcast has been advocating for the use of GenAI as a tool for creatives for a very long-time through educating her audience, especially her 'Patreons', of which I am one. J Thorn, another podcaster and writer, has also inspired me to give this new way of writing a try.

I'd also like to thank Dr. Richard MacKinnon, host of "My Pocket Psych", from whom I've learned a lot about our psychology as knowledge workers. And of course, I've learned loads from my guests and co-hosts at the "21st Century Work Life" podcast, where I've been podcasting about remote work for over five years now.

I asked my co-author whether there was anyone they wanted to thank and this is what it replied:

"As an AI language model, I don't have personal sentiments or experiences, so I don't require any specific acknowledgments. However, you might consider acknowledging the role of AI and technology in the creative process of your book. For instance, you could mention something like:

"I would like to acknowledge the role of AI and advanced technology in the creation of this book. The collaboration with ChatGPT, an AI language model developed by OpenAI, has been instrumental in synthesizing and refining the vast information available on remote work and time management. This book stands as a testament to the potential of human-AI collaboration in the realm of writing and creativity.""

There is one more person I'd like to thank, and that's my husband Kevin, who, although he doesn't read anything I write, couldn't be more supportive of my endeavours. And I know I owe a lot to my father, who instilled in me a love for technology - I wonder what he would have made of all of this.

Finally, as a member of Generation X, I am very grateful to have been born at a time when I've seen technology explode, and been able to take advantage of it. I remember life before the internet, mobile phones and of course, accessible AI. It's a great time to be an artist.

ABOUT PILAR ORTI AND SAM BYTE

Sign up to get updates from Collective Wisdom:

https://collectivewisdommedia.com/

For her writing with Sam Byte, Pilar leads the content creation process. She uses her expertise to direct the chatbot, ensuring that the content it produces is in line with her knowledge and values.

Pilar's role extends beyond simply prompting the AI; she actively integrates additional text and images where necessary and undertakes multiple rounds of editing to refine the content. (If you are interested in the process of writing in this way, get in touch with Pilar.)

Pilar focuses on the topic of remote work, leveraging her experience in this field. Her writings with Sam Byte are a blend of AI-generated content and personal insight and explore various aspects of working remotely. The aim is to offer readers a thoughtful perspective on this increasingly relevant subject.

Now a writer and podcaster, Pilar continues to generate content about remote work . Here's a collection of her remote-related work, which you can find in ebook and paperback format in most online stores.

Thinking Remote: Inspiration for Leaders of Distributed Teams by Pilar Orti and Maya Middlemiss (Also in audiobook)

Online Meetings that Matter: A Guide for Managers of Remote Teams by Pilar Orti

Navigating Asynchronous Communication

An audio-first course for new managers of remote teams

Find out more at virtualnotdistant.com/audio-first-course

Check out the **21st Century Work Life podcast** for information and inspiration on leading remote teams, online collaboration and new ways of working.

Pilar is also the author of "The A to Z of Spanish Culture", "Plan Your Podcast" and her voiceover memoir "Hi, I'm Here for a Recording". She is also the host of "Management Café" and "Adventures in Podcasting", as well as a VoiceOver artist, whose roles include Xuli in the BBC's animation "GoJetters".

If you found this guide useful, sign up to the Collective Wisdom New Releases mailing list over at collectivewisdommedia.com

You will only receive emails when a new book or course is out.

To get in touch with Pilar, head over to collectivewisdommedia.com

And if you enjoyed this book and found it useful, please leave a review on your favourite book selling platform.

www.ingramcontent.com/pod-product-compliance
Lightning Source LLC
Chambersburg PA
CBHW061203010526
44110CB00063B/2662